The LOVEABLE *You*

What Matters Publishing House

IVAN TAIT

www.WhatMattersMM.org

Copyright © 2022 Ivan Tait

All rights reserved. Except as permitted under the U.S. Copyright Act of 1976, no part of this publication may be reproduced, distributed, or transmitted in any form or by any means, or stored in a database or retrieval system, without the prior written permission of the publisher.

Unless otherwise indicated, all Scripture quotations are from ESV® Bible (The Holy Bible, English Standard Version®), copyright © 2001 by Crossway, a publishing ministry of Good News Publishers. Used by permission. All rights reserved.

Scripture quotations taken from the Amplified® Bible Classic, Copyright © 1954, 1958, 1962, 1964, 1965, 1987 by The Lockman Foundation
Used by permission. (Www.Lockman.org)

Scripture quotations marked HCSB are taken from the Holman Christian Standard Bible®, Used by Permission HCSB ©1999,2000,2002,2003,2009 Holman Bible Publishers. Holman Christian Standard Bible®, Holman CSB®, and HCSB® are federally registered trademarks of Holman Bible Publishers.

Scriptures marked KJV are taken from the KING JAMES VERSION (KJV): KING JAMES VERSION, public domain.

Scripture taken from The Message. Copyright © 1993, 1994, 1995, 1996, 2000, 2001, 2002. Used by permission of NavPress Publishing Group.

Scripture quotations taken from the (NASB®) New American Standard Bible®, Copyright © 1960, 1971, 1977, 1995, 2020 by The Lockman Foundation. Used by permission. All rights reserved. Www.Lockman.org

Scripture quotations taken from The Holy Bible, New International Version® NIV®, Copyright © 1973 1978 1984 2011 by Biblica, Inc. TM, Used by permission. All rights reserved worldwide.

Scripture taken from the New King James Version®. Copyright © 1982 by Thomas Nelson. Used by permission. All rights reserved.

Scripture quotations marked (NLT) are taken from the Holy Bible, New Living Translation, copyright ©1996, 2004, 2015 by Tyndale House Foundation. Used by permission of Tyndale House Publishers, Carol Stream, Illinois 60188. All rights reserved.

Scripture quotations marked TPT are from The Passion Translation®. Copyright © 2017, 2018, 2020 by Passion & Fire Ministries, Inc. Used by permission. All rights reserved. ThePassionTranslation.com.

Published by What Matters Ministries and Missions Publishing

ISBN   979-8-9856155-3-1

Design and Layout: What Matters Ministries and Missions

Printed in USA

CONTENTS

INTRODUCTION..5
63 LOVEABLE TRUTHS.......................................7
THE TRANSFORMATION LIFE........................87
THE BROKEN LIFE..94
THE REPENTANCE LIFE................................104
THE VINE LIFE...116
THE WORD LIFE...128
THE CRUCIFIED LIFE....................................139
THE WORSHIP LIFE.......................................150
THE DECISION LIFE......................................163
PARTNER WITH IVAN...................................173

INTRODUCTION

Looking back, I can recall the lovable people who have affected my life. The most impactful of them all was my mother—with her kind words and the way she would hold my hand and tell me I was her favorite (and to be sure not to tell my brothers and sisters). I recall the kindness in her eyes, the softness of her smile, and the admiration and pride with which she spoke of me to everyone. I felt unique and special in the midst of wolves. She could calm me with her love-language—her endearing terminology for me. She never raised her voice or shouted at me, *not one time* in my life. She never missed a sports event or neglected to tell me I was gifted and special. My mother's love kept me safe from the demons of life—the hateful people all around me who rejected, persecuted, and abused me. She was the lighthouse, the voice crying in the wilderness.

There is a better, kinder way to live—a path of goodness, paved with goodwill and the refusal to take revenge. I hope you are like me and have had someone lovable in your life: a protector of your hope, a guardian of your goodness, someone reminding you that there are gracious and kind people in your life, who is a true model of Christlikeness, someone without meanness or a vengeful spirit, a deeply safe and lovable soul—a dove in the midst of snakes and scorpions. Or perhaps as you read this small offering, you find yourself swallowed by feelings of loneliness and without friends. Perhaps life has twisted your expectations and bent your perceptions. Perhaps you look around and find yourself alone, rejected, and unsought. You realize that you have burned too many bridges and lost too many friends and relationships. Your heart has been broken again and again. You realize that no one feels comfortable around you. You are never invited to anything. You spend your days in regret, asking yourself what you did to get here. Surely they can see your efforts, but they don't. You have your companions: pain and broken hopes.

May I give you some hope? Being loved is about being lovable. Anyone, with God's help, can become lovable. The Bible gives us many insights, such as in

Proverbs 18:24, which says in effect, "If you want lots of friends, show yourself friendly." In *The Lovable You*, I will endeavor to guide you to the wells of insight. Do not quit, do not lose hope, and do not grow weary in your faith. There is a melting place where you dissolve and are remade with God's graces—such as authenticity, genuine love, compassion, goodwill, and forgiveness. You will discover many sacred secrets in this book. You will lose your old, rejected, unloved identity, and will be reborn to the ways of lovable goodness. I will take you on a new and healing journey to find and create the lovable you. You may not be able to change people, but you certainly don't have to drive them away. Dare to hope that in the very near future, you will be so lovable, so attractive, so love inspiring, that you will have more friends than you know what to do with. You will be someone's hiding place, someone's heart medicine, someone's torch of truth. Dare to believe that the best is yet to come!

LOVABLE PEOPLE WILLINGLY SUFFER FOR YOU

To suffer for another is to heal them. When someone is selfless for you without resentment, you honor them. You appreciate their love offerings. Suffering is the fruit of someone who sees value, divine worth, and a unique purpose for your life. To suffer for someone and believe it is your honor to do so is to give feet to Christlikeness. Suffering is pain, which equals transformation, and transformation equals the comprehension of Jesus Himself. To be a true friend, you must suffer for each other. You must die daily and hurt daily. Be brave enough to love enough to transform pain into medicine. Lovable people feel your pain and are willing to eat it for you. They say, "Give me your pain. I will be hurt by it so that you don't have to be." This is true beauty on display. Lovable people do not consider how pain will change them. They just know that their love cannot do anything less. Their beauty is in their fearless willingness to embrace the cross for you.

FOR YOUR TRANSFORMATION:

Romans 8:18 TPT	2 Timothy 3:12	1 Corinthians 10:13
Revelation 21:4 NIV	Philippians 3:10-11 NIV	
Psalm 119:71 NKJV	1 Peter 4:13 NIV	

2 LOVABLE PEOPLE NEVER GOSSIP OR BETRAY YOUR CONFIDENCE

Lovable people are beautiful because they know how to be true to their word. They protect your failures and weaknesses. They hide your guilt under a cloak of mercy. They *cannot* betray a friend or enemy; they have seen the devastation of betrayal. They have felt the hurt of trusting and being used, rejected, and violated. Lovable people are full of beauty because they never spread the ugly pieces of you all over the world. They do not share negative information that would defame your character. You love them because they paint you with a brush of kindness. People who can be trusted with your privacy are worthy of your trust and love. Even when offended, they remain faithful. They are true to themselves, they merit respect, and they are magnets of honor and friendship.

Lovable people hold your secrets as sacred trusts, gems of honor. The inner beauty of lovable people is like a blooming garden, one without weeds. They are picked, pulled, and cultivated souls sprouting the fragrances of Heaven. You feel protected by their loyalty. You feel honored by the absence of malice in their actions. You sense their loving value for you and you melt. They remind you of all the pain you could have avoided if you had been loved by those born to protect you. You feel appreciated by their discernment and harbored by the price they have paid to be lovable.

FOR YOUR TRANSFORMATION:

Proverbs 16:28 NIV   Proverbs 20:19 NKJV   Ephesians 4:29 NASB

Proverbs 11:13 NIV   Proverbs 19:16 NKJV

Proverbs 18:8 NASB   1 Timothy 5:13

LOVABLE PEOPLE KNOW WHAT MAKES YOU FEEL LOVED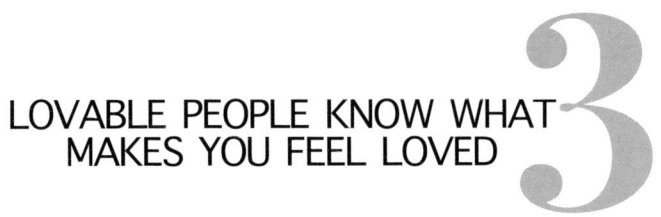

To know an unspoken need is to be one with God. To see the invisible pain in a crushed spirit is to be in tune with God. To hear a broken spirit and locate its brokenness is to have your divine hearing unlocked. Lovable people somehow find your love channel. They can sense what makes you feel loved. They practice making you feel loved. Those who can make you feel loved are master artists of the soul. They use your soul like a canvas upon which they can draw the beauties of God. With every stroke of their paintbrush, they serenade your pain away. They know which colors scare you and make you fearful. They only use the colors of love as seen and felt by you. Lovable people are beautiful because you do not need to train them how to treat you. They are the ambassadors of goodwill and healing arts. When they finish with you, your scratches and tears are no longer visible.

FOR YOUR TRANSFORMATION:

Psalm 119:130 TPT   Proverbs 14:29 NASB   Proverbs 2:2-5

Colossians 4:6 NKJV   Proverbs 3:13-19 NKJV

Proverbs 4:7   Psalm 37:4

4 LOVABLE PEOPLE ARE NOT JEALOUS OR ENVIOUS TOWARD YOU

Beauty is void of envy, for it is its own mirror, reflecting the face of God. When you encounter it, you are filled with hope that you can be loved, appreciated, and celebrated by someone. It is a very empowering feeling to try without resistance, to attempt and fail without fear. The beauty of lovable people is their ability to embrace your success without signs of remorse. Beautiful people love your ascension; they get as much joy out of your success as they do out of their own. No one can resist the beauty of genuine goodwill. Beautiful people make you the object of their happiness. When you are blessed, they are blessed. When you succeed, they succeed. When you are promoted, they are promoted. These character traits glue your soul to them. They are not fair-weather friends; they truly love to see goodness chase you. They are always praying for your good fortune. Lovable people are committed to seeing your life bettered. They remember from where they have come, and they see your heart; they feel your hurts, and they know your dream's enemy is their *archenemy*. Jealousy is viewed as a curse. They sleep with a clear conscience by empowering others, and they empower themselves. They erase the memories of slavery to insecurity. They place a gold wreath upon your head.

FOR YOUR TRANSFORMATION:

James 3:16 NASB   Proverbs 27:14 TPT   1 Corinthians 3:3 TPT

Galatians 5:19-21   Romans 12:2 NASB

Job 5:2 NASB   Proverbs 19:5 NIV

LOVABLE PEOPLE ARE NOT RUDE OR OFFENSIVE

Rude people are selfish people. Offensive people are defiant people. People who control their mood are loving. People who refine their reactions are considerate. Lovable people work hard at purging their parasites of rudeness. They actively cultivate goodness-responses based on an inner drive to heal others.

Lovable people are beautiful because they see you, feel you, hear you, and understand you. They work hard at measuring pain and painful responses. They see the world around them and categorize divinity, and they apply divinity to loneliness. They are beautiful to you because they take your rudeness and love you *through* it. They do not define you through it. They ignore the cries of your selfishness and refuse to agree with your former view of yourself. They choose God for you even when you don't. They know that rudeness is a lie and that offensiveness is a twisted cry to be in control of your uncontrollable pains. They understand that *kind patience* produces eternal fruit. They see your future once you are touched by love. They feel and walk on the egoless path. No vanity rules their emotional life. They observe equality by demanding your freedom.

FOR YOUR TRANSFORMATION:

Matthew 5:16 NASB   Luke 17:2-3 NASB   1 Peter 3:16 NIV

Ephesians 2:3 NASB   James 3:13 NASB

Ecclesiastes 8:5 NKJV   1 Peter 2:13 NASB

THE LOVABLE JESUS

When Jesus saw his mother and the disciple whom he loved standing nearby, he said to his mother, "Woman, behold, your son!" Then he said to the disciple, "Behold, your mother!" And from that hour the disciple took her to his own home.

John 19:26-27

LOVE BREAKS THROUGH EVEN IN THE MIDST OF TERRIBLE PAIN; IT SEES OTHERS' NEEDS AND DOES NOT CONSIDER ITSELF!

6
LOVABLE PEOPLE ARE CONSIDERATE AND CLEAN

To lose self-care is to partner with the lower desires of the Adamic nature. Self-care reveals the voices that are mentoring you. You lose your identity because you don't feel loved. Someone who is routinely loved also loves. Consideration is a heart searching for significance. To consider is to put the needs of others before your own. Time with Jesus produces cleanliness—outward and inward. Lovable people know the raptures of divine cleansings. They understand the workings of the Holy Spirit on the naked heart. They understand that dirt equals death and dirtiness equals separation from the holiness of God. The inconsiderate dwell in their entitlements; others do not matter to them. They *presume* their way to exclusion, they *assume* their way to loneliness, and they *covet* their way to spiritual poverty. Lovable people are beautiful to you because they prepare for you. They spend time being beautiful, attractive, and pure. They know that cleanliness draws holiness. Purifications are badges of honor. To be clean in all facets is to make room for the Presence of God.

FOR YOUR TRANSFORMATION:

Isaiah 1:16 NIV   Psalm 51:10 NIV   Psalm 51:7 NASB

2 Corinthians 7:1 TPT   1 John 1:9 TPT

Deuteronomy 23:13-14   Ezekiel 36:25 NASB

7
LOVABLE PEOPLE ARE NOT COMPETITIVE

Competition creates an opponent—someone to beat, challenge, and outplay. To compete for the Kingdom and take it from someone is the spirit of an insecure thief, not a loving, gracious doer of good deeds. What is attractive about lovable people is that they don't compete with you. They are so secure in themselves that they are not striving to gain, win, or get what you have. They have achieved completeness. They know that God will supply all of their needs and that in trusting Him, they will obtain all that belongs to them. Every prosperity, every wealth, every cherished gem of life—all of it is perfectly prepared, safeguarded, and protected for them. They are lovable because they treat you like family, not a competitor. They do not practice coveting, greed, or jealousy.

They love seeing you win, even if it means they lose. People like this can be trusted by God to handle His treasures. Lovable people live to serve your destiny. They never make you feel afraid of them or suspicious of their motives. They spread the beauty of genuine goodwill toward you. Lovable people see your need for validation and success. They try to always fill the hollow places of your soul. Anyone who behaves this way will always be loved by someone, somewhere.

FOR YOUR TRANSFORMATION:

Matthew 5:9 MSG	Romans 12:18	Matthew 7:12 NASB
James 3:17-18 NASB	Colossians 3:15 TPT	
1 Thessalonians 5:13 NASB	Romans 14:19 TPT	

LOVABLE PEOPLE NEVER MAKE JOKES ABOUT YOU

There is no mocking in lovable people. You are not fair game for ridicule and shaming. They do not go behind your back and tell jokes about you. They do not practice ripping your soul open. They do not enjoy eating your pain. They do not gather insecurity stones and hurl them at you like your soul and heart are made of iron. Lovable people have learned that to diminish you is to diminish themselves. To trivialize you is to make themselves as small as an ant, with no spine or character. The beauty of lovable people flows from their honor for the hearts of others. They cherish your feelings, and you can let down the gates of your heart's citadel. You are illuminated by the sincerity of their goodness. They love love. They worship God and Him alone. They shelter you by covering you. They keep your soul hidden from the spears of your enemies by continually encouraging you with words of self-healing and emotional well-being. To be able to cherish another is worth the gold of Heaven.

FOR YOUR TRANSFORMATION:

Romans 12:10 NIV   Hebrews 13:1 NIV   1 John 4:20 MSG

John 13:34 NASB   John 15:13 NKJV

1 John 4:7 TPT   1 John 3:18 TPT

9 LOVABLE PEOPLE KNOW HOW TO READ AND GUARD YOUR EMOTIONS

Misreading people is how we practice suspicion. Misdiagnosing people is how we assign blame. To rightly read a soul is to guard and cover their emotions. Lovable people are experts of protection. They guard you. They are living, walking shields. They stand in front of the enemy's arrows; they break the arrows of judgment, and the arrows of self-doubt are dissolved. They replace hopelessness with undeniable inspiration. They know what to say and precisely how to say it without being coached. They know if you are emotionally unreasonable. They know if you have impure filters and are blinded by pain. They aim at resolving, not blaming. Their goal is solution, not exclusion. They are beautiful because they have the gift of divine sensitivity. You love them because they cover you in safety, security, and peace. Lovable people do not need a course in caring. They are masters of bonding.

FOR YOUR TRANSFORMATION:

Luke 7:47-50   2 Kings 4:26   Isaiah 30:18 NASB

John 2:5   Hebrews 5:7 NIV

John 20:15-16 NIV   Isaiah 40:1-2 TPT

10
LOVABLE PEOPLE NEVER LIE TO YOU; THEY KINDLY SPEAK THE TRUTH

A kind truth wounds the right way. A word spoken at the right time delivers the soul from many torments. Words covered in the oils of healing are welcomed, even if they hurt. Truth must be managed by an expert wordsmith. Truth without love is a sledgehammer that crushes the soul and evicts the hope of change. Lovable people never dishonor others by honoring lies. Those who habitually lie are dishonorable. Lovable people protect your future by telling you the truth about today. Liars are in line to inherit from their mentor, the Father of Lies. Lovable people are beautiful because they care too much to create an atmosphere of suspicion. They heal the atmosphere by filling it with beautiful and ugly truth. They wipe out confusion, they illuminate doubt, and they abolish insecurities. They are what we all wish to be—trusted by God.

FOR YOUR TRANSFORMATION:

Proverbs 12:22 NIV   Proverbs 19:9 NIV   Psalm 101:7 NIV

Proverbs 12:19 NIV   Luke 8:17

John 8:44   Ephesians 4:25 TPT

THE LOVABLE JESUS

One of the criminals hanging beside him scoffed, "So you're the Messiah, are you? Prove it by saving yourself—and us, too, while you're at it!"

But the other criminal protested, "Don't you fear God even when you have been sentenced to die? We deserve to die for our crimes, but this man hasn't done anything wrong." Then he said, "Jesus, remember me when you come into your Kingdom."

And Jesus replied, "I assure you, today you will be with me in paradise."

Luke 23:39-43 NLT

YOU CANNOT INSULT LOVE; IT REACHES OUT INTO THE DARKEST SOUL—AND SAVES TO THE UTTERMOST.

11
LOVABLE PEOPLE ARE TRUSTING; THEY ARE NOT UNNECESSARILY SUSPICIOUS

To trust someone is to give them a sacred gift. To have that trust betrayed is sometimes to lose that person forever. Trust is the cement for every long-lasting relationship. Trust is the glue that keeps the holy bond between husbands, wives, and children. Without trust, all Hell is released in confusion, fear, doubt, anger, unforgiveness, and bitterness. Lovable people give their trust even when it is not deserved. They see genuine repentance. They perceive the birth of goodwill. They know the value of new beginnings. They have failed and have been rescued by mercy. They judge how they desire to be judged. The lovable resurrect hope by believing in you when no one else will. They save you from your own man-made gallows. And they remove the hangman's noose from your neck and give you a gift wrapped in trust.

FOR YOUR TRANSFORMATION:

Proverbs 3:5 TPT   Psalm 56:3-4 NLT   Jeremiah 29:11 NKJV

1 John 4:18 MSG   Psalm 37:5 TPT

Mark 11:24 NIV   Psalm 40:4 TPT

12 LOVABLE PEOPLE DO NOT BREED WORRIES IN YOU

Worry addicts dishonor God. They believe the promises of Satan. They are addicted to the power of fear, not faith. Worry is how you tell God that you do not trust His plan for your life. Worry is a mind terrorist and a faith assassin. Worry steals your God-given dreams. Lovable people have ended their conversation with worry. They have chosen the path of faith. They see what Moses saw—Him who is invisible. They jump when God says, "*Jump.*" They risk their lives for the Gospel. Lovable people know how to extract worry from your mind. They aid your faith by defying your worries with the Bible's promises. For every worry, there is a promise pillow. The beauty of lovable people is that they lead you to the house of God's reassuring comforts.

FOR YOUR TRANSFORMATION:

Philippians 4:6-7 TPT   1 Peter 5:7 NIV   Matthew 6:25

Proverbs 12:25 MSG   Psalm 94:19 NKJV

Psalm 125:1-2   Matthew 6:33-34 NIV

13 LOVABLE PEOPLE DISCOVER THE KIND OF FRIEND YOU NEED AND BECOME THAT

Friendship is the medicine of the broken soul; it drives the identity predators away. Divine friendship is like washing your soul with faith soap. Lovable people learn the kind of friend they need to be for you and become that, as long as it leads to the arms of God. To become medicine, you must know the medicines of God. You must have inside information on the healing acts of Jesus. You love the lovable person because they are able to untangle your soul. They become ladders to God, sure and steady rungs of the ladder leading to Him. They are not given to fragile love. They are not heralds of self-serving. They transform into paths of deliverance, places of divine escape, and anchors of hope. Lovable people are not imprisoned in their unbending ego. You love them because they come to you dressed in unconditional acceptance.

FOR YOUR TRANSFORMATION:

Proverbs 18:24   John 15:3 TPT   Ecclesiastes 4:9-10

Proverbs 17:17 NLT   1 Corinthians 15:33 NASB

1 Thessalonians 5:11   Proverbs 27:9 NIV

14 LOVABLE PEOPLE ENJOY SERVING WITHOUT COMPLAINING OR RESENTMENT

To serve the ungrateful makes you worthy of washing the feet of Jesus. Servants wash feet with their character. Their towel is their unflinching commitment to your success. Their water and its basin is the ability to see beauty and worth hidden in the darkest places of your life. Their greatness washes the worthlessness out of you. Their humility in the face of your indignity stirs you into repentance. Their unreasonable and undeserved commitment to love you compels you to become worthy of their faith in you. Their beauty shocks you. It opens your heart, prying its sealed doors and ripping them off their thousand-year-old hinges. Oh, what beauty they show—beauty that only Jesus could have revealed to them! For them, there is no complaining, no resentment, and no heart-betraying attitudes—there is only undaunted and selfless serving.

FOR YOUR TRANSFORMATION:

Mark 10:45 TPT   Ephesians 6:7 MSG   1 Peter 4:10 NASB

Romans 12:11 TPT   Galatians 5:13 NIV

Matthew 23:11 TPT 1 Peter 4:11 NIV

15
LOVABLE PEOPLE DON'T CARE IF THEY GET CREDIT FOR WHAT THEY DO

To be great and refuse to reveal it is the face of Jesus. To quietly do and be the miraculous, and hide it in the closet of prayer, is beauty in action. Invisibility is the face of humility; invisible service yields the greatest rewards in Heaven. To accomplish greatness in the eyes of Heaven, you must disappear from the eyes of the ego life. Divine beauty is the mark upon the heart of truly lovable people. To work quietly behind the scenes, unnoticed, uncelebrated, and undemanding, is lovable; this is Christ's beauty shining out of the skin of divinity's touch. We stand in awe when someone refuses to take credit for beautiful things. We immediately trust these beautiful people. They resurrect our hope in humankind. A great deed done in secret rings the bells of Heaven through eternity.

FOR YOUR TRANSFORMATION:

Philippians 2:3-4 NKJV   Proverbs 22:4 NLT   Colossians 3:12 NIV

James 4:6 NLT   Proverbs 11:2 NIV

Proverbs 15:33 NLT   Micah 6:8 NASB

THE LOVABLE JESUS

Now as He was going out on the road, one came running, knelt before Him, and asked Him, "Good Teacher, what shall I do that I may inherit eternal life?"

So Jesus said to him, "Why do you call Me good? No one is good but One, that is, God. You know the commandments: 'Do not commit adultery,' 'Do not murder,' 'Do not steal,' 'Do not bear false witness,' 'Do not defraud,' 'Honor your father and your mother.' "

And he answered and said to Him, "Teacher, all these things I have kept from my youth."

Then Jesus, looking at him, loved him, and said to him, "One thing you lack: Go your way, sell whatever you have and give to the poor, and you will have treasure in Heaven; and come, take up the cross, and follow Me." But he was sad at this word, and went away sorrowful, for he had great possessions.

Mark 10:17-22 NKJV

LOVE IS TRUTH COVERED IN COMPASSION. IT WILL NEVER LIE OR MISLEAD; IT ALWAYS REVEALS THE PATH TO GOD!

16 LOVABLE PEOPLE ARE NOT OVERSENSITIVE OR TOUCHY

The overly sensitive practice witchcraft. They speak from their unhealed wounds and create atmospheres of fear. The overly sensitive violently take your eyes off of Jesus and onto themselves. They refuse the comfort of Heaven to receive the attention of the crowd. Lovable people hide their hurt and bring it to the feet of Jesus. They refuse to muddy the waters of life by washing you in their unforgiveness. The attraction of people with too much love for Jesus is their refusal to glorify rudeness, offensiveness, and ugliness. They catch pain and smother it to death with their graciousness, their refusal to expose the dysfunction in you. Rather, they pray and believe in your untapped potential. Lovable people are not a walking time bomb. They become impossible to offend. They refuse to turn ugly people's deeds into altars of worship.

FOR YOUR TRANSFORMATION:

Proverbs 16:32 NKJV   James 1:19-20 NLT   Proverbs 14:29 TPT

Proverbs 10:32 MSG   Ephesians 4:26 NLT

Ephesians 4:31 TPT   Psalm 103:8 NIV

17 LOVABLE PEOPLE ARE NOT LAZY AND SLOTHFUL; THEY THINK AHEAD

Laziness is the face of partnership with death. It is the addiction to the spirits of selfishness and every thief of the soul. To embrace slothfulness is to die a thousand deaths. Lovable people do more than is asked of them. They finish every task by lifting the bar of excellence. You ask them to do one thing, and they do 10. You inconvenience them over and over again, and they keep asking for more. They do not resent being taken advantage of. They are blind to your inconsiderate ways. They see not you, but God. They don't dwell in the here and now but in the places where Jesus lives and walks. You use them, and God prospers them. You abuse them, and God promotes them. You steal from them, and God hands them their inheritance. Lovable people cannot be wronged because God is watching over them and is handing them the true riches of Heaven.

FOR YOUR TRANSFORMATION:

Proverbs 13:4

Colossians 3:23 NASB

2 Thessalonians 3:10 NIV

Proverbs 10:4 NIV

Proverbs 18:9 NLT

1 Timothy 5:8 NKJV

Proverbs 6:7-11 NIV

18
LOVABLE PEOPLE TREAT ALL OF YOUR MISTAKES AS LIFE LESSONS, NOT PERMANENT DISASTERS

Mistakes are successes clothed in failure; they take away other false solutions. After you fail, you have one less path to take until you succeed. People who learn from their mistakes are on a path of permanent improvement. Lovable people know this about you, and they can communicate the truth to you about life and its struggles. Mistakes that go unchecked change your perspective into mind terrorists of guilt and self-accusation. Lovable people disarm your mistakes; they remove the permanence of failure. They help you see the journey you must walk with your own weaknesses and the secrets of overcoming yourself. Lovable people are beautiful aides in divine perspective. You love them because they empower you to keep walking divinely through the fields of landmines without the fear of permanent damage and disaster. The beauty of lovable people shines through when they take your failures and mistakes and turn them into stepping-stones of success and victory. They say, "Oh—that was an opportunity to end another area of failure and enter a new stage of wisdom and success!" Where failure is, silent beauty comes forth.

FOR YOUR TRANSFORMATION:

Ephesians 4:32 NKJV   1 John 1:9   Matthew 18:21-22 NIV

Mark 11:25 NLT   Matthew 6:14-15 TPT

John 14:27 NKJV   Psalm 119:104 NLT

19 LOVABLE PEOPLE APOLOGIZE AND CHANGE

Change is the evidence of God's Presence; it is the *only acceptable apology*. Change screams **love and hope** to those who have been hurt by your unmovable stubbornness. Lovable people are quick to apologize and quick to make permanent adjustments. They seize the opportunity to change. They aggressively pursue answers and solutions to their problems. They don't make excuses or walk in denial. They admit they are wrong and change their behavior. To see someone change is like seeing rain during a drought. Change is the most beautiful act of love you can give those you love; it is more than any explanation or reason you can give. It tells people that you deeply care about them. God sees change as an "I love you." You love people who alter themselves to heal you. Their change empowers the future. The transformed take the sword out of the hand of their accusers; they emerge out of the cocoon with Heaven's wings and beauties. A transformed frog who now looks like a majestic eagle is the hope of the world.

FOR YOUR TRANSFORMATION:

2 Chronicles 7:14 NLT   Acts 3:19 NIV   2 Peter 3:9

Acts 17:30   Matthew 3:8 TPT

Acts 11:18 TPT   Luke 5:32 NLT

LOVABLE PEOPLE PRAY FOR THOSE THEY LOVE AND THOSE WHO DON'T LOVE THEM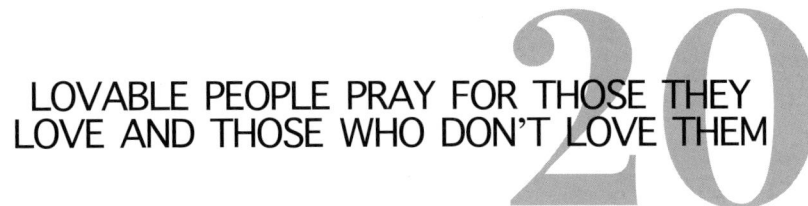

Whoever prays for their friends rescues their future. Whoever prays for their enemies gains new friends. When I know someone loves me enough to pray for me, I feel treasured and valued; those who love me with prayers save my view of myself. Prayer is faith partnering with answers; it is opening the windows of Heaven for others. To pray for someone you love is *goodness*; to pray for someone who doesn't love you is *divine*. True beauty is anything you do that blesses your enemies. I feel valued by people who ask God to help me become who He made me to be. I feel loved by people who invest their time, faith, and love into my life by praying for God to answer my prayers. Prayer changes reality; it is the great equalizer. Anyone can do it and reap its miraculous results.

Lovable people take time daily to pray for those who are hurting them, lying about them, and repeating lies about them. They pray for their salvation, blessing, and well-being. These are stars in a starless world and medicines in a sick world. Their beauty is faith inspiring and heals the memories of the world around us.

FOR YOUR TRANSFORMATION:

Matthew 5:44 NKJV   1 Thessalonians 5:17 NLT   James 5:16 TPT

Philippians 4:6-7 NLT   Ephesians 6:18 NIV

James 5:13 NASB   1 John 3:22 NLT

THE LOVABLE JESUS

They sailed to the region of the Gerasenes, which is across the lake from Galilee. When Jesus stepped ashore, he was met by a demon-possessed man from the town. For a long time this man had not worn clothes or lived in a house, but had lived in the tombs. When he saw Jesus, he cried out and fell at his feet, shouting at the top of his voice, "What do you want with me, Jesus, Son of the Most High God? I beg you, don't torture me!" For Jesus had commanded the impure spirit to come out of the man. Many times it had seized him, and though he was chained hand and foot and kept under guard, he had broken his chains and had been driven by the demon into solitary places. Jesus asked him, "What is your name?" "Legion," he replied, because many demons had gone into him. And they begged Jesus repeatedly not to order them to go into the Abyss. A large herd of pigs was feeding there on the hillside. The demons begged Jesus to let them go into the pigs, and he gave them permission. When the demons came out of the man, they went into the pigs, and the herd rushed down the steep bank into the lake and was drowned. When those tending the pigs saw what had happened, they ran off and reported this in the town and countryside, and the people went out to see what had happened. When they came to Jesus, they found the man from whom the demons had gone out, sitting at Jesus' feet, dressed and in his right mind; and they were afraid.

Luke 8:26-35 NIV

LOVE IS UNCONDITIONAL GOODNESS, CURING DEMONIC INSANITIES; IT BREAKS THE CHAINS AND FETTERS OF HOPELESS BONDAGE AS ALL ELSE FAILS. LOVE RE-CLOTHES THE SOUL WITH DIVINITY'S TOUCH!

21 LOVABLE PEOPLE ALWAYS POINT YOU TO JESUS

To arrive at Jesus is to have solved life's problems. Jesus *is* the destination of living. He *is* the cure of life, the salvation to all unsolvable problems. Jesus is the utopia of the soul. He is the Place all mankind is searching for. He is life itself, unflinching beauty wrapped in a living person. He is what every soul needs even when they don't know they need Him. He is the song of the brokenhearted that mends and heals your terrors and fears. He calms the anxieties of the faithless. He is the key that unlocks you, the peace that chases away the shadows in the night. He is the awe the heart cannot live without. He is the touch that changes destinies forever. Jesus, the window of life, a hope wrapped in a gift of love. Jesus is the well of the thirsty soul and the streams of the soul's deserts. Jesus is the cure for the ugliness of life's snake bites. He is the answer to the insanities of life. He breaks the chains of your DNA curses and cures the sickness of selfishness. Jesus—this is the One who stretches out His arms and welcomes the ravaged traveler into His family. Jesus—He is the only one who embraces the lepers of the world and turns them into royalty. This Jesus is the obsession of lovable people. They always stand as lighthouses, pointing the way to Him and away from the dangerous rocks and cliffs of the world.

FOR YOUR TRANSFORMATION:

Hebrews 12:1-2 NKJV

John 12:21 NIV

Revelation 19:13 NKJV

Isaiah 6:1 NASB

Revelation 14:1

Revelation 5:5 NASB

Hebrews 13:8 NKJV

22 LOVABLE PEOPLE DO NOT THROW PITY PARTIES

To feel self-pity when you have been given the keys to Heaven is to be a blind soul inside of the richest place on earth. Self-pity is the highest form of emotional insanity. How long do you have to feel sorry for yourself before it feels good? Self-pity denies God's goodness; it rejects the answers of Calvary and honors Satan's lies about life. Lovable people have emptied themselves of all self-pity. They do not wallow in the swamps of defeatism. They will not entertain your doubt, unbelief, or despair. They live on the victory side of Calvary. They are blind to hopelessness and self-doubt. They have cursed the idols of poverty and worldly thinking. They know and appreciate their God-given wealth. They are not in partnership with thieves. They love you by forcing you to appreciate what you have. They don't throw pity parties. They celebrate the answers before they manifest. Lovable people spread the beauties of appreciation and realized benefits. They are beautiful to you because they protect you from the blind beggar you sometimes think you are. Lovable people kill ungratefulness in its tracks.

FOR YOUR TRANSFORMATION:

James 1:5-6 NLT

1 Corinthians 16:13 TPT

1 Peter 5:8 NASB

Deuteronomy 31:6 NKJV

Joshua 1:9 NKJV

Job 17:9 MSG

Ephesians 6:10 NASB

23

LOVABLE PEOPLE ARE NOT FRAGILE AND INSECURE

Fragile love is insecurity trying to intimidate God. The fragile are already broken. They are allergic to pressure; they collapse in the face of resistance and stress. Fragile souls are walking accidents of emotions. Lovable people do not live at insecurity's door. They cannot be pressured into breaking. They can handle all your bad news and your reactions do not define them. They love without crashing, breaking, or hurting. Lovable people do not keep a record of wrongs suffered because they know that this behavior leads to feelings of control and guilt. The beauty of people you can't break is their gift of long suffering. Their power is in their grace with handling pain. They love you by not being your victim even when they could be. The insecure have made altars out of other people's criticisms. They have exalted naysayers into prophets, accusers into mentors, and rejectors into mirrors of truth. The insecure dwell in the mouth of self-doubt. Their food is the fear of failure. They behave like they cannot change. The beauty of lovable people is that they have silenced their false teachers, caged their lying mentors, and enslaved their tormentors. Beautiful people can be counted on even when you reject them. They know what you need: life—refusing-to-be-crushed, love-unbreakable, joy-undeniable, faith-conquering life!

FOR YOUR TRANSFORMATION:

Philippians 4:13 MSG   Isaiah 41:10 TPT   Exodus 15:2 NLT

Ephesians 6:10 NIV   1 Chronicles 16:11 NKJV

2 Timothy 1:7 TPT   1 Samuel 15:30 AMPC

24 LOVABLE PEOPLE PRIORITIZE YOU AND MAKE YOU FEEL LIKE IT IS THEIR PRIVILEGE TO HELP YOU

Whatever you prioritize mentors you. Whatever you prioritize changes you. Whatever you prioritize, you become. To be the object of someone's priorities is to be sculpted by grace. Priority is love; anything that matters comes first! When someone loves you enough to prioritize you, you feel like a treasure. Lovable people are experts at making you feel like you are their first priority. God makes you His first priority. His thoughts about you in one day are more than all the sand in all the oceans of the world. God's thoughts are medicines. To think like God is to be like God in the sense of His virtues and graces. Lovable people know that Christlikeness is total access to God, unlimited privileges, and irresistible beauties of the spirit. Lovable people will drop everything and focus their attention on you. They are not divided in their attention; they only see you. They treat you in such a way as to heal you with favor. They feel privileged to help you. They envy your company and convince you that you are worth their attention.

FOR YOUR TRANSFORMATION:

Romans 12:10 TPT   1 Peter 5:5 TPT   Colossians 3:12 NLT

Philippians 2:3 NIV   Ephesians 4:32 TPT

John 15:12 NASB   1 John 3:23 NIV

LOVABLE PEOPLE ARE POSSESSED BY SHOWING MERCY

Mercy is when you don't get what you deserve. Mercy is a second chance, but repeatedly. Mercy is how you write *your own* judgment. Mercy reunites you with your future, and those who practice mercy reveal the heart of God. Lovable people are the most nonjudgmental people in the world. No sin derails them, no failure drives them away, and no mistake—however ugly—turns them against you. They are the *irrational believers in* your destiny. Their acts of mercy save lives. They bring hope to broken, dysfunctional families. They tolerate the intolerable. Mercy guides their mind. They think with forgiveness. They decide with compassion. You love them because you know you are never a failure in their eyes. They redeem you with virtue. They bring you back to God by leaving the door of reconciliation permanently open. Oh, what glorious hope this word *mercy* is: to be forgiven over and over again!

FOR YOUR TRANSFORMATION:

James 2:13 MSG   Luke 6:36   Matthew 5:7 NASB

Matthew 9:13 NIV Hebrews 4:16 NKJV

1 John 1:9 TPT   1 Peter 1:3

THE LOVABLE JESUS

Now a woman, having a flow of blood for twelve years, who had spent all her livelihood on physicians and could not be healed by any, came from behind and touched the border of His garment. And immediately her flow of blood stopped.

And Jesus said, "Who touched Me?"
When all denied it, Peter and those with him said, "Master, the multitudes throng and press You, and You say, 'Who touched Me?'"

But Jesus said, "Somebody touched Me, for I perceived power going out from Me." Now when the woman saw that she was not hidden, she came trembling; and falling down before Him, she declared to Him in the presence of all the people the reason she had touched Him and how she was healed immediately.

And He said to her, "Daughter, be of good cheer; your faith has made you well. Go in peace."

Luke 8:43-48 NKJV

LOVE IS RELEASED BY UNREASONABLE FAITH—IT FLOWS WHEN WE REACH OUT TO JESUS WITH OUR LAST BREATH—THE TOMB IS OPENED AND WE LIVE AGAIN!

26
LOVABLE PEOPLE LOVE JESUS MORE THAN ANYTHING ELSE

To love Jesus is to save yourself. To love Jesus is to unlock the vault of Heaven. To love Jesus is to draw the death out of your soul. To love Jesus is to become one with perfection. Jesus' love, once obtained, ends the identity wars. When lovable people think, they first ask, "What would Jesus want me to do?" The answer, once revealed, is immediately obeyed without hesitation. Lovable people are beautiful because they are not double-minded. They do not shift like sand. They are "lifers." They are so committed to Jesus that you know they walk while carrying their anchor with them. They are not like clouds. They are not movable; they are not tossed like the waves of the sea. They are like the Rock of Ages—solid, reliable, and unmovable. They always take you to Jesus. They always lead you to the Rock that is higher than you. Jesus *is* their life. He is their sure foundation, and you trust them for that. Because they love Jesus so much, you always feel safe with them.

FOR YOUR TRANSFORMATION:

Luke 7:37-38

John 14:21 TPT

Matthew 6:24 MSG

Deuteronomy 6:5 MSG

1 John 3:1 NASB

Acts 21:13 NIV

1 John 4:19 NASB

27 LOVABLE PEOPLE DO NOT EMBARRASS YOU IN PUBLIC

To shame a loved one is to partner with Satan's opinion of them. Love never embarrasses anyone. Love never puts on display the flaws or faults of another. People who embarrass you on purpose have become your accusers. Lovable people cannot help anyone mock you; they guard and protect your identity. They nourish your God-given image. They help define you with celebration and encouragement. They prop you up with affirmation. This is why you love them. They are your fans, your cheerleaders. They are guaranteed celebrators of your life. To embarrass or shame you is a loathsome thing to them. Lovable people do not tamper with your sense of being. They heal it and enlarge it. Lovable people are lovable because your flaws are safe in their hands. Their beauty is great because anyone can possess it. Anyone can be inwardly beautiful and outwardly radiant. Lovable people remember when they were publicly embarrassed. The sting of the mocker leaves a visible scar. Lovable people make it their aim to remove that scar forever.

FOR YOUR TRANSFORMATION:

Matthew 7:12 MSG   Romans 12:10 NLT   Exodus 20:12 NIV

Titus 2:7 TPT   1 Corinthians 11:22

Leviticus 19:32 NIV   1 Thessalonians 5:12-13 NKJV

28
LOVABLE PEOPLE DWELL IN THE PRESENCE OF GOD

The greatest gift you can give someone is the Presence of God. The Presence of God changes your heart by tenderizing it. The Presence of God is the hospital of God. Wherever the Presence of God is, a miracle follows. Lovable people practice dwelling in His Presence; they carry Him like a living cure for all of life's ailments. Lovable people bring peace, scatter fear, dissolve anxiety, and drive away torment. Lovable people bring you into the Presence of God, where you are *defined*. The Presence of God is the heart of God on display. Lovable people know that without His Presence, no good thing can be born. Lovable people are always praising, praying, and worshiping God. They have excommunicated complaining, profanity, and negative talk. They are atmosphere cleansers. Their spirit is sweet and they spread it to you. They sing songs all day long, breaking the spirit of heaviness off of you. Those who dwell in the Presence of God have no enemies and see no predators.

FOR YOUR TRANSFORMATION:

Psalm 16:9-11 NLT   Exodus 33:14 NKJV   Psalm 31:20 TPT

Psalm 100 NKJV   2 Chronicles 29:11 AMPC

Psalm 27:8 NLT   Acts 3:20-21 NLT

29 LOVABLE PEOPLE GIVE WITHOUT WANTING ANYTHING BACK

There is a beauty to generosity. There is a clarity that comes from being free from possessions. To be able to give away anything is to be invisible. You cannot be bribed, seduced, threatened, or intimidated. You will not sell out or be bought. You are God's, and no other master can own you. This is freedom: to have everything and own nothing, to need nothing and yet possess all things. Generosity is the banner of lovable people. They give without wanting anything back. They open their hearts and live their lives with open hands. Lovable people leave you richer than they found you. To the generous, there should be no poor people. Lovable people have learned to heal others through generosity. They have learned to make dreams come true by paying for them. Lovable people never feel that they deserve more than you—quite the opposite. They feel honored by meeting *your* needs. You are the victims of their Christlike generosity. Your dreams come true, your needs are met, your power is increased, your resources are multiplied, and your heart is enlarged to be like them.

FOR YOUR TRANSFORMATION:

Acts 20:35

Proverbs 22:9 TPT

2 Corinthians 9:7 NIV

Luke 6:38 TPT

2 Corinthians 9:11 NLT

2 Corinthians 9:6 NKJV

Deuteronomy 15:10 MSG

LOVABLE PEOPLE DON'T BRING UP ANYTHING THAT HURTS YOU

Memories are the gasoline of the predators and emancipators. Memories reopen wounds or close them forever. Memories are to be burned and forgotten if they are hurtful, or celebrated and rehearsed if they are pleasant. Some people use the past to imprison your present, yet others use your past to put chains on your future. Lovable people are not the keepers of your painful and ugly memories. They lead you to the well of miracles where you, like the woman at the well, can find forgiveness for a past full of mistakes. They come to visit you with God's divine eraser; they permanently wipe away the pain in your memory. They make sure to talk you out of the past and into the future by never rehearsing your failures. With lovable people you start at 100, not at 0. Lovable people know what hurts you. They bring the oil and wine of restoration and heal you with it. They show you compassion, bandage your memories, and treat your wounds. They remove the dirt and wash your soul with love. They take you to God in prayer and pay your debts by reminding you that everyone begins at the same broken bridge—and they stay with you until you are ready to travel life's road again.

FOR YOUR TRANSFORMATION:

2 Timothy 2:23-25 NASB   Proverbs 10:12 TPT   Proverbs 16:28 MSG

Proverbs 20:3 MSG   James 3:14-16 NLT

Proverbs 26:20 NIV   Proverbs 6:16-19 TPT

THE LOVABLE JESUS

Soon a Samaritan woman came to draw water, and Jesus said to her, "Please give me a drink." He was alone at the time because his disciples had gone into the village to buy some food. The woman was surprised, for Jews refuse to have anything to do with Samaritans.

She said to Jesus, "You are a Jew, and I am a Samaritan woman. Why are you asking me for a drink?"

Jesus replied, "If you only knew the gift God has for you and who you are speaking to, you would ask me, and I would give you living water."

"But sir, you don't have a rope or a bucket," she said, "and this well is very deep. Where would you get this living water? And besides, do you think you're greater than our ancestor Jacob, who gave us this well? How can you offer better water than he and his sons and his animals enjoyed?"

Jesus replied, "Anyone who drinks this water will soon become thirsty again. But those who drink the water I give will never be thirsty again. It becomes a fresh, bubbling spring within them, giving them eternal life."

"Please, sir," the woman said, "give me this water! Then I'll never be thirsty again, and I won't have to come here to get water."

"Go and get your husband," Jesus told her.

"I don't have a husband," the woman replied. Jesus said, "You're right! You don't have a husband—for you have had five husbands, and you aren't even married to the man you're living with now. You certainly spoke the truth!"

"Sir," the woman said, "you must be a prophet. So tell me, why is it that you Jews insist that Jerusalem is the only place of worship, while we Samaritans claim it is here at Mount Gerizim, where our ancestors worshiped?"

Jesus replied, "Believe me, dear woman, the time is coming when it will no longer matter whether you worship the Father on this mountain or in Jerusalem. You Samaritans know very little about the one you worship, while we Jews know all about him, for salvation comes through the Jews. But the time is coming—indeed it's here now—when true worshipers will worship the Father in spirit and in truth. The Father is looking for those who will worship him that way. For God is Spirit, so those who worship him must worship in spirit and in truth."

The woman said, "I know the Messiah is coming—the one who is called Christ. When he comes, he will explain everything to us."

Then Jesus told her, "I am the Messiah!" Just then his disciples came back. They were shocked to find him talking to a woman, but none of them had the nerve to ask, "What do you want with her?" or "Why are you talking to her?"

The woman left her water jar beside the well and ran back to the village, telling everyone, "Come and see a man who told me everything I ever did! Could he possibly be the Messiah?" So the people came streaming from the village to see him.

John 4:7-30 NLT

LOVE QUENCHES THE ETERNAL THIRST— IT RECREATES THE SOUL—IT BREAKS THE MEMORIES OF REJECTION. LOVE ENDS THE WAY OF FAILURE!

31 LOVABLE PEOPLE AREN'T PEOPLE-PLEASERS

People-pleasers are traitors in Christian suits; they cannot be loyal to God because their loyalty is to people. People-pleasing is a form of idolatry—the exaltation of man above God. People-pleasers have chosen their masters. They see man's approval as the ultimate reward for living. Lovable people do not walk with those chains. They please God first. He is their anchor, sail, rudder, boat, and captain. Their allegiance is to pleasing the spoken and unspoken desires of God. Lovable people are beautiful because they cannot be influenced by what anyone thinks. They are opinion blind; they cannot hear the objections of the world. They live by a sacred code: to please God is life. To lovable people, God's will *is life*. God's will is the safest place to live. Lovable people lead you to the hiding place of divinity, the secret place of light and truth, the place where no shadows exist. Lovable people's beauty is their single-heartedness to God and to you. They cannot be talked out of being your friend. They say with their actions, "You are worth more than all the cheap friends in the world." And that is pure gold!

FOR YOUR TRANSFORMATION:

Galatians 1:10 TPT   1 Thessalonians 2:4 NLT   Proverbs 29:25 NKJV

Matthew 10:28 NLT   2 Corinthians 10:12 MSG

Matthew 23:28 TPT   Colossians 3:22 NASB

32
LOVABLE PEOPLE ARE VERY ACCEPTING OF PEOPLE WHO THINK DIFFERENTLY THAN THEY DO

A friend is a true friend even when you disagree. To accept what you disagree with is to love beyond the flaws. Jesus loved you while you were yet a sinner. It is what glues you to Him. Because He loves you just as you are, you worship Him. Lovable people love people who live and think differently than they do. There is a grace to giving respect to someone you believe is wrong. People who make those they disagree with feel worthy are mind doctors. They are idea geniuses, people who can think like God. Every thought of God produces a miracle, and every miracle solves an impossible problem. Lovable people make people feel like their ideas are worth listening to and researching. They are not mockers or ridiculers of the unwise, ignorant, and foolish. They have the grace to help define the minds of the untapped. Lovable people have the beauty of not being intimidated by ideas and thoughts that contradict theirs. They are intellectually happy in their persuasions. They have tested, proven, and retested everything in the foundation of their life. Only what has been purified in the furnace of God can stand the test of holy fire. Only the pure intellectual gold can accommodate God.

FOR YOUR TRANSFORMATION:

2 Timothy 4:1-2 NLT   Ephesians 4:2 NLT   Romans 14:1-4

John 8:7 NASB   Acts 10:28 TPT

Matthew 7:12 TPT   Proverbs 17:15 MSG

33 LOVABLE PEOPLE ARE NOT SELFISH OR GREEDY

Selfishness is self-worship; it exalts the primitive design of the flesh and its own self-relevance. Selfishness is the curse and cause of all of mankind's evils. To feed selfishness is to partner with death. Selfishness is the source of every type of harm. Every betrayal, every abuse, every robbery, every lie, every lust, every greed, every coveting, every broken vow, every abandonment, and every self-gratification has its origin in selfishness. Selfishness is lovable people's conquered foe. They have removed its voice, pulled its teeth, and blinded the eyes of its greed. Lovable people are not in covenant with self. They are beautiful because they have mastered the spirit of inconvenience. They use inconvenience like a crowbar to open your heart with the wonders of a life ruled by selflessness. Selflessness is so beautiful because it is rooted in giving to others what you could hold for yourself. Selflessness is so shocking in the world we live in that we are surprised by anyone sacrificing or inconveniencing themselves for us. We are, therefore, healed by simply beholding the kindness and wondering what and where such beauty comes from. Selflessness is pain retrained to serve Heaven.

FOR YOUR TRANSFORMATION:

1 Timothy 6:10 NIV   Proverbs 28:25 NLT   1 Timothy 6:9 NLT

Luke 12:15 TPT   Hebrews 13:5 NIV

Proverbs 15:27 TPT   Matthew 6:24 TPT

34 LOVABLE PEOPLE PRAY ENOUGH TO BE CHANGED

Prayer that transforms counts. Prayer that removes something evil is divine. Prayer that erases a tormenting memory is a medicine. Prayer that reveals the face of God takes away all the monsters of the mind. For lovable people, prayer is a chance to cure the sicknesses of their friends. True prayer warriors are the sword of God cutting the heads off your enemies while you sleep. Prayer warriors are God's snipers picking off the Devil's assassins hiding in the trees. Lovable people know how to pray change into their lives. They have purged the selfish, impure motives from their lives and opened the gates of answered prayer. Prayer clothed in unselfish generosity is beauty. Lovable people have a beauty of intimacy with God; their nearness to Him brings you to Him. Transforming prayer is the source of the transformed life. Lovable people *are* prayer; they do not practice it. They have become a living, breathing expression of prayer. Their lives pray, and God blesses you because of it!

FOR YOUR TRANSFORMATION:

2 Corinthians 3:18 NKJV   2 Corinthians 5:17 NIV   Romans 12:1-2 NASB

Psalm 17:15 MSG   Galatians 2:20

Psalm 51:10-12   1 John 3:2-3 NLT

35 LOVABLE PEOPLE FIND WAYS TO BE INSPIRING

Without inspiration, no one would attempt the impossible. And without the impossible, no one would dare to be brave or heroic. Without heroes, the world would devour itself. Inspiration is the food that the spirit needs to defeat all of the enemies of life. Inspiration is God thinking for mankind. Inspiration silences fear and doubt; it crushes the insecurity of your mind, then ejects it. It sets you on God's rocket and launches you into the stratosphere. With inspiration, you can be anyone your faith tells you that you can be. With inspiration, you are unafraid to try to fly when all you've ever done is crawl. Inspiration is lovable people's gift to you; they cover you in it. They speak it, sing it, live it, and tell stories about it. No one can reach God without the ladder of His inspiration. God is the ultimate Inspirer. His words have set the world on fire. His thoughts have healed a hundred generations. His inspirational life has captured the minds and hearts of thousands of nobles, atheists, and kings. He alone possesses eternity in His words and in His eyes. He who once sees Jesus is never the same again. From the richest to the poorest, from the lowliest to the greatest, from the wisest to the most foolish, He has won the heart of the world. Lovable people know and live this.

FOR YOUR TRANSFORMATION:

1 Samuel 17:51 NLT   Daniel 6:20 NLT   Joshua 6:20 NLT

Joshua 14:11-12   Joshua 1:9 NKJV

1 Chronicles 28:20 MSG   Proverbs 28:1 MSG

THE LOVABLE JESUS

After these things there was a feast of the Jews, and Jesus went up to Jerusalem. Now in Jerusalem, by the Sheep Gate, there is a pool which in Hebrew is called Bethesda, having five porticoes. In these porticoes lay a multitude of those who were sick, blind, limping, or paralyzed. Now a man was there who had been ill for thirty-eight years.

Jesus, upon seeing this man lying there and knowing that he had already been in that condition for a long time, said to him, "Do you want to get well?"

The sick man answered Him, "Sir, I have no man to put me into the pool when the water is stirred up, but while I am coming, another steps down before me."

Jesus said to him, "Get up, pick up your pallet and walk." Immediately the man became well, and picked up his pallet and began to walk.

John 5:1-9 NASB

LOVE ENTERS THE UNREASONABLE BELIEVER. WHEN WE REFUSE TO SETTLE INTO OUR PARALYZED LIVES, LOVE REAPPEARS WITH ITS HEALING HANDS!

36 LOVABLE PEOPLE PAY THEIR OWN WAY AND NEVER USE OR TAKE ADVANTAGE OF OTHERS

Self-sufficient people are a burden-lifting gift. The self-responsible never add to the worry of the day. They never bring their burdens with them. They are not freeloaders or beggars. They love you by carrying their weight *and* yours. Their hand is never stretched out without having something in it to give away to others. Lovable people lift burdens; they do not create them. Lovable people have learned how to carry the weight of the world without being weighed down. The more you give them to do, the stronger they get. They feed on need. They love to deliver the oppressed. They love to carry the weary on their shoulders. The heavier the soul, the more powerful the deliverance. Lovable people pay their way; they are the paymasters of life. Everywhere they go, debts dissolve and needs are met. The poor become rich, the rich become rich with God, and the poverties of life are eradicated forever.

FOR YOUR TRANSFORMATION:

Colossians 3:23 NLT   Proverbs 16:3 TPT   1 Corinthians 10:31 TPT

Proverbs 18:9 TPT   Genesis 2:15 NLT

2 Thessalonians 3:10 NKJV   Proverbs 14:23 MSG

37 LOVABLE PEOPLE ARE NOT POSSESSIVE OR SOCIALLY DEMANDING

The possessive are tyrants in training. The demanding are the slaves of selfish pride and human inequality. The possessive believe the world was made to serve and please *them*. Lovable people put wings on others and then help them launch their dreams. Lovable people cannot be demanding because they don't need anything that anyone has. The Lord is their Shepherd. They don't lack; therefore, they don't demand. Lovable people do not smother or control. They make room where there is no room. They enlarge the space around people by never practicing verbal or physical witchcraft. They empower; they don't diminish. They equip; they don't strip. They supply; they don't steal. They create answers, not questions. Lovable people are the most comfortable people to be around. There is no choking around them—no suffocating looks, actions, or gestures. Lovable people break chains; they don't put them on people. Lovable people come carrying the trumpet of liberation!

FOR YOUR TRANSFORMATION:

Titus 3:2 NLT   Psalm 18:35 TPT   Ephesians 4:2 TPT

Proverbs 15:1 NLT   Proverbs 25:15 NASB

Colossians 3:21 NKJV 1 Peter 1:22 NIV

38 LOVABLE PEOPLE ARE NOT RACIST, BIASED, OR TRIBAL

There are no racists in Heaven. Racism is the ego deceiving itself. Racism makes God out to be a racist. Racism is the denial of the artistry of God. All humans begin with the seed of innocence and are, therefore, potential temples for a holy God. Racists wish to be exalted by hating all who are not of their uniqueness. Lovable people treasure unlovable people. Lovable people know that God is not colorblind; He is color-coordinated. He does not erase our colors, but celebrates them. To be human is to be divinely loved. John 3:16 says, "For God so loved the world, that he gave his only Son, that whoever believes in Him should not perish but have eternal life." Lovable people have perfected the art of *unbiased love*. To lovable people, no one is without priceless beauties; but they must be uncovered from the rubble of abuse. Lovable people believe that each of us is priceless because we are worth whatever God was willing to pay for us. If God paid with Jesus and Jesus is God, then we are worth what God is worth. And that is the value placed on every human who has or will ever live. The beauty of lovable people is that they see you as more valuable and beautiful than themselves without being diminished or insecure. They are expert valuers!

FOR YOUR TRANSFORMATION:

Acts 10:34-35 NIV   James 2:1 NLT   Romans 2:11 NIV

James 2:4 NLT   1 Timothy 5:21 NKJV

Proverbs 28:21 MSG   Galatians 3:28 MSG

LOVABLE PEOPLE HAVE A SPIRIT OF CONTENTMENT

To be content is to have conquered the world and all of its temptations. Contentment is perfect soundness of knowing. Contentment is the absence of coveting and greed. Contentment is the soul in a state of divine grace. Contentment is the heart knowing that it is perfectly loved. Contentment is the mind perfectly persuaded of its divine value and worth. To be content is to have become perfectly satisfied with Jesus and His plan for your life. Lovable people are walking libraries of contentment. They ooze with completeness. Their soul has no identity leaks. Their mind has no broken-down boundaries. Their heart has no open, infected wounds. They do not build altars to their abusers. They are not still searching for purpose and meaning. They have found the fountain of youth, and it is life inside of Jesus. Lovable people make you feel as if anyone with the keys to the Kingdom can find contentment and everlasting life while still living here on earth. Lovable people's beauty is their romance with the divinities of God. Contentment is the fruit of time alone with the tangible Presence and voice of God!

FOR YOUR TRANSFORMATION:

Philippians 4:11-12   1 Timothy 6:6 MSG   2 Corinthians 12:10 TPT

Luke 3:14 NLT   Hebrews 13:5 NLT

Psalm 17:15 NLT   Psalm 63:5 TPT

40 LOVABLE PEOPLE HAVE A GIFT FOR DISSOLVING UNHAPPINESS

How many times have you been with lovable people when they drove your blues away? Their personality changes the color of the world; it adds the colors of joy that are missing from your day. They are not moody, emotionally driven people. They smile when you can't. They laugh and take the permanence out of unhappy circumstances. Lovable people have learned how to be happy as a habit and not as a response to perfect circumstances, treatment, or success. They are lovable because they always seem like they love life. Aim at this. Dissolve unhappiness. Make it your aim, your calling. Make it your ministry to drive away the gloomy clouds around the people you love. Cheer them, lift them, calm them, turn their sorrows into opportunities of deliverance and breakthrough. Be that person whom people can expect to unfurl their wings rather than trim them. You are called to be lovable by making the world a place in which God lives, where He rules the lives of His children, where He gets involved in the day-to-day activities of His family. Psalm 37:4 says, "Delight yourself in the Lord, and he will give you the desires of your heart." And Ecclesiastes 3:12 says, "I perceived that there is nothing better for them than to be joyful and to do good as long as they live." Be happiness, and happiness will follow you all the days of your life.

FOR YOUR TRANSFORMATION:

Proverbs 17:22 TPT   Proverbs 25:11 NLT   Proverbs 18:24 NKJV

John 3:29 NIV   Proverbs 15:1

Isaiah 52:7   Daniel 6:3-4 NKJV

THE LOVABLE JESUS

When Mary arrived and saw Jesus, she fell at his feet and said, "Lord, if only you had been here, my brother would not have died." When Jesus saw her weeping and saw the other people wailing with her, a deep anger welled up within him, and he was deeply troubled. "Where have you put him?" he asked them. They told him, "Lord, come and see." Then Jesus wept. The people who were standing nearby said, "See how much he loved him!" But some said, "This man healed a blind man. Couldn't he have kept Lazarus from dying? Jesus was still angry as he arrived at the tomb, a cave with a stone rolled across its entrance. "Roll the stone aside," Jesus told them. But Martha, the dead man's sister, protested, "Lord, he has been dead for four days. The smell will be terrible." Jesus responded, "Didn't I tell you that you would see God's glory if you believe?" So they rolled the stone aside. Then Jesus looked up to heaven and said, "Father, thank you for hearing me. You always hear me, but I said it out loud for the sake of all these people standing here, so that they will believe you sent me." Then Jesus shouted, "Lazarus, come out!" And the dead man came out, his hands and feet bound in graveclothes, his face wrapped in a head-cloth. Jesus told them, "Unwrap him and let him go!"

John 11:32-44 NLT

LOVE IS NEVER LATE—IT KNOWS WHEN TO OPEN THE TOMBS OF OUR LIVES, IT DEFIES THE LAWS OF NATURE, AND IT IGNORES THE PROTESTS OF DOUBT AND UNBELIEF!

41 LOVABLE PEOPLE KNOW PAIN AND HATE IT ON OTHERS

Lovable people are intimately connected with the monsters of pain. They have been embraced by sorrow and heartache. They have tasted rejection and changed it. They have been mocked and became celebrators. They have had vicious rumors told about them and sent back prayers of mercy. They have heard the echoes of abandonment and refused to feel like castaways. They have been betrayed and did not become betrayers. They have had arrows of blame shot at them and did not take revenge. They have felt the cold hand of cruelty and absence of mercy and yet chose to remain loyal and faithful. They have suffered wrongfully and unjustly and did not blame God. The lovable are masterpieces of surrender to the welcoming ways of God. You, too, can be lovable. Take your pain and place it at the feet of Jesus. Release your sorrows to Heaven. Unbind yourself from the shackles of regret. Push away remorse, banish resentment, and cast away self-pity. Instead, remind yourself that the steps of good people are ordered of the Lord (Ps. 37:23). He makes all things beautiful in His time (Eccles. 3:11). He will never leave you, nor forsake you (Deut. 31:6). He is always there for you (Ps. 23:1), and in Him there is victory (Rom. 8:37).

FOR YOUR TRANSFORMATION:

1 Corinthians 13:7 NLT   Romans 13:10 TPT   Isaiah 53:5 TPT

Jeremiah 40:4 NKJV   Jeremiah 30:8 NIV

Matthew 11:28-29 NASB   Psalm 55:22 TPT

42
LOVABLE PEOPLE ACT GRACIOUSLY WHEN THEY ARE INCONVENIENCED

I remember as a child growing up in my mother's home, watching my stepfather lose his temper and let profanity fly when his meals were not ready or when the TV would break. He was an ugly man with no tolerance or regard for other people's feelings. Lovable people have learned that inconvenience is the stairway to Christlikeness. They know that every inconvenience brings a reward of the Presence of God. They know that loving people when it is inconvenient opens new rivers of God's tangible Presence. The lovable do not throw fits when they are asked to do something inconvenient. Neither would Jesus. I can imagine Jesus and how often in a day people asked Him to do inconvenient things. He always handled it with gracious selflessness. Now you can call on the inner wells of selflessness living inside of you. You can be that person whom people are not afraid to ask for help, that person who makes people feel like their lives matter.

Lovable people are lovable because they are not the slaves of inner passions and appetites of selfish urges and impulses. Remember, "Let each of you look not only to his own interests, but also to the interests of others," (Phil. 2:4). "Do good, and lend, expecting nothing in return, and your reward will be great, and you will be sons of the Most High, for He is kind to the ungrateful and the evil," (Luke 6:35). "Do nothing out of rivalry or conceit, but in humility consider others as more important than yourselves." (Phil. 2:3 HCSB).

FOR YOUR TRANSFORMATION:

Colossians 3:17 TPT	1 Peter 3:15 TPT	Philippians 2:14-15 NKJV
Proverbs 17:22 NKJV	Philippians 4:8	
Proverbs 15:1 MSG	1 Peter 4:1 MSG	

43 LOVABLE PEOPLE ARE NOT HABITUAL CONFRONTERS

If you have ever known a habitual confronter, you know that it is hard to feel comfortable and at ease with them. The atmosphere changes from light and happy to serious and stressful; they suck the joy out of the room. Lovable people do not make mountains out of molehills. If you want to be lovable, be the person who can confront *without accusing, blaming, or condemning.* Lovable people are lovable because they have mastered the art of lifting the spirits of those around them. They take the fear out of the room. They call in the Holy Spirit. They are light-hearted, joy-giving, hope-filled people. Mistakes are opportunities to learn, grow, and succeed, not a time to reject, divorce, or annihilate. Lovable souls are gentle correctors—kind executioners, loving disciplinarians. Lovable people use goodness as their rod, mercy as their instruction, and gentleness as their pruning tool. They confront while healing. They create an expectation of hope in the corrected. They remember that discipline seems painful rather than pleasant but that it yields the peaceable fruit of righteousness (Heb. 12:11). They know that a soft answer turns away wrath (Prov. 15:1), and that whoever loves discipline, loves knowledge (Prov. 12:1). They remind themselves that whatever any man reaps, he sows (Gal. 6:7-9) and that he who listens to reproof loves intelligence (Prov. 15:32).

FOR YOUR TRANSFORMATION:

Matthew 5:5 MSG   Titus 3:2 TPT   Matthew 11:29 TPT

James 3:13 NLT   Numbers 12:3 NKJV

Psalm 16:9-11 NASB   Romans 12:14

LOVABLE PEOPLE LIVE SURRENDERED TO GOD NO MATTER WHAT ANYONE ELSE DOES

Lovable people feed at God's table of surrender. They have mastered the art of a surrendered will. As the Lord Jesus said, "not my will, but Yours, be done" (Luke 22:42). They are not bullies. They do not push their way in or force their beliefs and opinions on others. They have a beautiful respect for people's freewill and opinions. They do not use guilt trips or emotional blackmail. They do not threaten or give ultimatums. They are ever kind, flexible, and accommodating. The lovable love because they have found the sacred ground of a conquered and surrendered will. They are fed by liberating, not imprisoning. They are nourished by sounding the bells of freedom and the trumpet of emancipation. Lovable people free you to choose life or death. They drink from the rivers of saying, "yes" to God's will. They remember that the surrendered prove what is the good, acceptable, and perfect will of God (Rom. 12:1-2). They recall that those who abide in God bear much fruit (John 15:6-7). They know that if they humble themselves under the mighty hand of God, they will be exalted in due time (1 Pet. 5:6). They believe that if they give their heart to God, their eyes will behold His ways (Prov. 23:26).

FOR YOUR TRANSFORMATION:

Romans 12:1 Luke 9:23 NASB Philippians 4:13 NLT

Philippians 2:5 NIV Romans 8:28 NASB

John 13:35 TPT James 4:8 TPT

LOVABLE PEOPLE REVEAL THE LOVE OF GOD TO YOU THROUGH ACTIONS

Not everyone has experienced the love of God. It was this very experience that caused me to be born again. While in high school as a 17-year-old, a good person gave me a Bible to read. It was an old, worn, shredded book with no cover. It had been written in and did not look like a sacred book. I had never read the Bible, as we were always told not to do so. But God had prepared a place for me, and as I read 1 Corinthians 13, "the love chapter," tears began to flow as if someone had opened the rivers of Heaven. I wept until there were no more tears. I tangibly felt the love of God, and it marked me for life. From that one experience, my whole life has been designed. Lovable people are lovable because they dwell in love. They have learned how to abide in love (John 15:4). They have tasted the intimacies of God (Ex. 25:22). They have bathed in the light of Heaven's glory (2 Cor. 4:6). They have seen the face of God (Ps. 17:15). They have touched the sacred and had the cheap removed (Ex. 3:2). They have entered the holy place, built their home there, and refused to leave (Heb. 6:18-19). Lovable people bring others into their piece of Heaven!

FOR YOUR TRANSFORMATION:

Matthew 5:16 TPT   Ephesians 2:10 NIV   James 2:14-17 NASB

James 2:26 NASB   Hebrews 13:16 NLT

John 15:13 TPT   Galatians 6:9 NKJV

THE LOVABLE JESUS

And behold, a woman in the city who was a sinner, when she knew that Jesus sat at the table in the Pharisee's house, brought an alabaster flask of fragrant oil, and stood at His feet behind Him weeping; and she began to wash His feet with her tears, and wiped them with the hair of her head; and she kissed His feet and anointed them with the fragrant oil. Now when the Pharisee who had invited Him saw this, he spoke to himself, saying, "This Man, if He were a prophet, would know who and what manner of woman this is who is touching Him, for she is a sinner."

And Jesus answered and said to him, "Simon, I have something to say to you."

So he said, "Teacher, say it."

"There was a certain creditor who had two debtors. One owed five hundred denarii, and the other fifty. And when they had nothing with which to repay, he freely forgave them both. Tell Me, therefore, which of them will love him more?"

Simon answered and said, "I suppose the one whom he forgave more."

And He said to him, "You have rightly judged." Then He turned to the woman and said to Simon, "Do you see this woman? I entered your house; you gave Me no water for My feet, but she has washed My feet with her tears and wiped them with the hair of her head. You gave Me no kiss, but this woman has not ceased to kiss My feet since the time I came in. You did not anoint My head with oil, but this woman has anointed My feet with fragrant oil. Therefore I say to you, her sins, which are many, are forgiven, for she loved much. But to whom little is forgiven, the same loves little."

Then He said to her, "Your sins are forgiven."

And those who sat at the table with Him began to say to themselves, "Who is this who even forgives sins?"

Then He said to the woman, "Your faith has saved you. Go in peace.""

Luke 7:37-50 NKJV

LOVE CANNOT BE DEFILED BY THE DEFILED. IT LIFTS THE BOUND, IT REGENERATES THE USED AND ABUSED, AND IT REPLACES THE STOLEN DIGNITY OF THE FORSAKEN!

46. LOVABLE PEOPLE ARE HABITUALLY GOOD TO YOU

The Bible praises people who attain goodness and goodwill. Lovable people are full of goodness toward others. They are not jealous, envious, or coveting. Lovable people have seen the goodness of God and desire to give it to the world. Their mind works through good thoughts. They always believe the best of people. They use goodness as a hook to capture the souls of the violated and slowly mend the tears, cure the infections, and bandage the open sores in the soul. Lovable people are good at heart. The question is, are you? Do you see good or bad? Trash or treasure? Worthless or priceless? Love or hate? Spoiled or ripe? Life or death? This reveals the kind of heart you have. You can be good. You can think like a good person. Goodness in people helps the badness in people. Your destiny is written in good deeds and good-heartedness. All the memorable people who have changed me have done so by their goodness. Lovable people are able to access the goodness of God. They remember that goodness and mercy shall follow them all the days of their lives (Ps. 23:6). They know that the fruit of the Spirit is goodness (Gal. 5:22). They believe that the goodness of God leads people to repentance (Rom. 2:4). They see that they shall look upon the goodness of God in the land of the living (Ps. 27:13). They gather goodness and remind themselves that God will make all His goodness pass before them (Ex. 33:19).

FOR YOUR TRANSFORMATION:

Psalm 23:6

Psalm 31:19 NLT

Psalm 34:8 TPT

Romans 2:4 TPT

Psalm 27:13 NKJV

Romans 12:9 NASB

Galatians 6:10 MSG

47 LOVABLE PEOPLE DESPISE SEEING EXPLOITATION

Lovable people will not tolerate exploitation of the orphan and the widow. They cannot stand the abuse of the innocent. Lovable people live their lives to rescue, to break chains, and to give freedom to captives. There is a spirit of rescuing in the heart of the lovable. Their first impulse is to protect the injured and to cover the unprotected. Lovable people will never abandon you; they stay in the foxhole with you. What good friends these people make! Faithful to the end, loyal, and true, they epitomize the friend who sticks closer than a brother. Lovable people have felt the suffering of being afraid and unsafe, and they would never want that for anyone. You, too, can be this. Lovable people protect instead of uncover, shield instead of pierce, and buffer instead of wound. They are love in action, kindness on display. They protect with their attitude, their perfectly-timed words, and their joy-filled personality. Being a protector is like speaking for God. He wants you safe. Lovable people remember that you shall not mistreat the innocent (Ex. 22:22). You shall rescue the orphan and the widow (James 1:27). They know that God will not leave us as orphans (John 14:18). They believe that they should learn to do good, seek justice, correct oppression, bring justice to the fatherless, and plead the widow's cause (Isa. 1:17). And they know that they should give justice to the weak and fatherless and maintain the right of the afflicted and the destitute (Ps. 82:3).

FOR YOUR TRANSFORMATION:

Matthew 25:40 TPT   Psalm 140:12   Ephesians 6:4

Hebrews 13:3 NLT   Zephaniah 1:9

Isaiah 1:17 NASB   Psalm 146:7 TPT

48. LOVABLE PEOPLE SHOW YOU COMPASSION BY FEELING YOUR PAIN

Compassion is sometimes mistaken for empathy. The difference between empathy and compassion is action. Feeling sorry for someone is self-centered and useless if no healing or rescuing takes place. The lovable feel your pain, and that makes them safe. Beware of those who cannot feel your pain; many times they will cause it. Compassion is the highest goal; to be moved to action is the most beautiful trait. Compassionate people have no timetable. They stay and stay and stay. They live by total devotion to your recovery. The richest soul is a soul with many compassionate friends. To achieve this virtue is to walk inside the heart of God. Compassion-driven souls leave healed people in their wake. Compassion is everlasting divinity wrapped in action and filled with purity. Compassion is the badge of being lovable. Stretch out your heart to God and ask Him to fill you with rivers of compassion. Compassion draws godly friends like pollen draws bees. Lovable people remember that being kind, tenderhearted, and forgiving leads to the nearness of God (Eph. 4:32). They know that Jesus lived by the food of compassion (Mark 6:34). They understand that compassion unlocks Heaven (Col. 3:12-13) and they see that living in compassion fulfills the law of Christ (Gal. 6:2).

FOR YOUR TRANSFORMATION:

Ephesians 5:1 TPT   1 John 3:17 TPT   Hosea 6:6 NLT

Psalm 145:8 NKJV   Psalm 103:13 NIV

2 Kings 13:23 MSG   Psalm 86:15 NASB

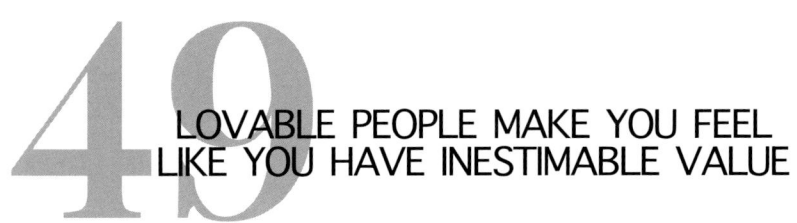
49 LOVABLE PEOPLE MAKE YOU FEEL LIKE YOU HAVE INESTIMABLE VALUE

Lovable people have had the devaluing removed from their heart. They are value minded. They sample Heaven's feasts by making you feel priceless. They enter the Presence of God through healing the worthlessness hiding inside your identity. They serve up a banquet of divine food by feeding lost causes. They find treasures in watching the forsaken restored. They are hospitals and cures walking around on Earth. Surely this is what we should strive for in our divine dependence on God. Surely, this is the call that wakens your heart to beauty in action. The lovable see with a different set of eyes. They dream of healing, miracles, and unexplainable wonders. Lovable people are irresistible pieces of Heaven who are let loose on earth to bring sanity to life's insanity. You are called and you are being called to surrender to your destiny to be a lovable, irresistible soul, one who sprinkles the world with angel dust, allowing your footsteps to be bridges from darkness to light. To the lovable, *there are no worthless people*—just undiscovered masterpieces waiting to happen. The lovable remember that you are worth whatever God was willing to pay, and He paid with Christ, so **you are worth what God is worth** *to Himself*. Whatever you believe is your value, that will be your valuing (Rom. 5:8). Lovable people know that you are worth more than all the sparrows (Matt. 10:31), and that you are the apple of God's eye (Zech. 2:8, Ps. 17:8) and a royal diadem (Isa. 62:3).

FOR YOUR TRANSFORMATION:

Psalm 139:13-16 NASB   Ephesians 1:4 NLT   Romans 5:8

Genesis 1:26-27   Ephesians 1:3 TPT

John 1:12 TPT   John 3:16 TPT

LOVABLE PEOPLE TREAT YOU LIKE AN HONORED GUEST DESPITE YOUR PAST

How you make someone feel, especially when they know you are aware of the wrong things they have done, is very revealing. How you treat people you don't like reveals how close you are to God. Lovable people are always aware of the shame and guilt others may have, and they work hard at removing it. They are firm believers in giving second chances. They see the future potential in you. They make you feel that you are worthy of honor and dignity. They walk in divine shoes and hand out dignity. They help you crush demeaning beliefs about yourself and destroy satanic, debilitating self-doubt. They fight for you with their respect, honor, and graciousness. They never fight or stand in confrontation. They yield, give way, and bless those who mistreat them. These are lovable people, the true salt of the earth. To be honored is to be healed. They clothe your spirit with royal robes of love and value. They dignify your existence and define your place in God's design. They remember that they should treat others as they want to be treated (Matt. 7:12). They know that it is necessary to honor people in order to honor God (Heb. 13:1-4). They believe that love should heal, restore, and repair, and that honor is medicine (Rom. 13:1-7). They understand that without honoring, all words are empty (1 Tim. 1:5).

FOR YOUR TRANSFORMATION:

Isaiah 43:18-19 NLT   Philippians 3:13-14 NIV   Psalm 103:12 NKJV

Romans 8:1 TPT   Luke 9:62 NIV

Matthew 6:14-15 NIV   Isaiah 43:25 NASB

THE LOVABLE JESUS

As He went on His way to Jerusalem, it occurred that [Jesus] was passing [along the border] between Samaria and Galilee. And as He was going into one village, He was met by ten lepers, who stood at a distance. And they raised up their voices and called, Jesus, Master, take pity and have mercy on us! And when He saw them, He said to them, Go [at once] and show yourselves to the priests. And as they went, they were cured and made clean. Then one of them, upon seeing that he was cured, turned back, recognizing and thanking and praising God with a loud voice; And he fell prostrate at Jesus' feet, thanking Him [over and over]. And he was a Samaritan. Then Jesus asked, Were not [all] ten cleansed? Where are the nine? Was there no one found to return and to recognize and give thanks and praise to God except this alien? And He said to him, Get up and go on your way. Your faith (your trust and confidence that spring from your belief in God) has restored you to health.

Luke 17:11-19 AMPC

LOVE DOES NOT ACKNOWLEDGE THE HANDIWORK OF SATAN—IT IS UNMOVED BY THE UNCLEAN JOURNEYS OF LIFE—IT PURIFIES; IT CLEANSES TO THE DEEPEST WOUND!

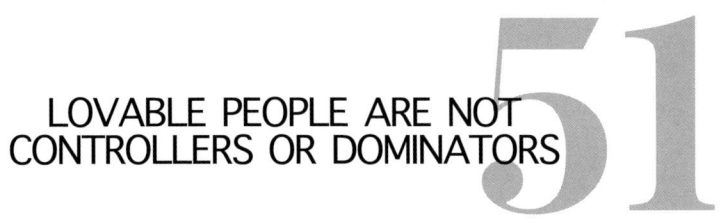

LOVABLE PEOPLE ARE NOT CONTROLLERS OR DOMINATORS

To control is to become a tyrant over someone you do not own. Controllers are vanity-led people. Controllers remove faith and trust from their lifestyle; they rob God of His ability to perform miracles. Controllers practice manipulation tactics by intimidating and bullying the weak and kind. Lovable people have a sense of injury. They know by their spiritual senses when someone is hurt, is going to be hurt, or could be hurt. They feel danger. They detect the arrows of cruelty and stop them any way they come. They hate cages, despise emotional prisons, and live to set people free. They are beautiful because they have *suffered* their way to beauty. They have taken their imprisonments and turned them into ministries of liberation. They are lovable because they are aware of you even when you are not. They remember that it was for freedom that Christ died (Gal. 5:1). They know that if the Son sets you free, you are free indeed (John 8:36). They see that where the Spirit of the Lord is, there is freedom (2 Cor. 3:17). They understand that the Devil comes to steal, kill, and destroy, but Jesus came to give us life and that more abundantly (John 10:10). They feel the powers of divine accomplishments—that if anyone is in Christ, they are a new creation (2 Cor. 5:17).

FOR YOUR TRANSFORMATION:

Titus 3:2 MSG   Proverbs 15:1   2 Timothy 2:25-26 NLT

James 3:17 TPT   Ephesians 4:2 NIV

Philippians 4:5 TPT   Isaiah 40:11 NASB

52 LOVABLE PEOPLE ALWAYS PREFER YOU BEFORE THEMSELVES

Putting others before yourself is an act of faith in God. Preferring others is the essence of the divine nature. Preferring others' desires, wants, and wishes before yours releases the powers of your divine nature. To habitually prefer others is to stay connected to the Presence of God, to be fed by God Himself—for Jesus lived a preferring life. From the first day to the last day, He did everything for you to save you, restore you, heal you, deliver you, mend you, and cure you. The lovable always think of you before they think of themselves. They have unlocked the treasures of the preferring life—secrets that are unexplainable. They can only be felt and experienced. The lovable are beautiful because they see the value in others' voices. They enhance the beauties of looking outward instead of inward. They work first and last without needing to be noticed. They care because you are their love project. The lovable are beautiful to themselves only when you are truly beautiful to them. They remember to love you and show you value by honoring you and outdoing you in giving respect (Rom. 12:10). They know not to do anything from rivalry or conceit but in humility to count others more significant than themselves (Phil. 2:3). They understand that true wealth comes from giving from a pure motive and a sincere heart, not from compulsion or fear (2 Cor. 9:7). They see that God sees the heart before the act (1 Sam. 16:7).

FOR YOUR TRANSFORMATION:

Romans 12:10   Philippians 2:3   Ephesians 4:32 NLT

Ephesians 4:1-2   John 15:12

1 Peter 1:22 NASB   1 Corinthians 13:3-7 MSG

LOVABLE PEOPLE SPEND THEIR TIME TRYING TO HEAL YOU

You love them because they always bring medicine with them. They leave the pain and heartaches at home. They detect your wounds and always have the right prescription. They know what to check in your vital signs, where to apply pressure, where to operate, where to bandage, what to cut out, and what to pour in—the oil and wine of the Holy Spirit. They are hospitals. They breed recovery by their kind manner. Their beauty is in their harmlessness. No one will ever say of them, "They are dangerous." They will never be accused of hardness or insensitivity. They always have time for you, always make room for you, and always set a place for you on the table of their heart. There are no ghosts in their soul, no haunted personalities, and no unresolved pain. They have walked through the swamps of their life with Jesus and drained it. They have become a doctor, nurse, and surgeon all in one, for they love you. They remember that we become partakers of the divine nature by *believing and practicing* the promises of God (2 Pet. 1:4). They know that the nearness of God is our health (Ps. 73:26). They understand that our bodies and souls are the temple of the Holy Spirit (1 Cor. 6:19-20). They see the value in healing and restoring others (Luke 10:9). They value health and treat it as wealth (3 John 2). They take people and make them better (Luke 10:30-34). They are ever vigilant in their pursuit of divine healing powers (Jer. 30:17).

FOR YOUR TRANSFORMATION:

Colossians 3:13 NLT   Galatians 6:2 NKJV   Galatians 5:13 TPT

John 15:17 NIV   1 John 4:11 NASB

1 Peter 3:8 MSG   James 1:27 TPT

54 LOVABLE PEOPLE CARESS YOUR HEART WITH FRIENDSHIP

There is a beauty in the caressing of a heart, especially a broken and dysfunctional one. There is a divinity to people who can locate your heart and fix it in a matter of minutes or hours. To caress the heart is to resurrect hope. To caress the heart is to receive the divine heartbeat within you. To caress the heart is to collect the tears of fear and pain and work them out. The beauty of lovable people is that they do not fear your pain. They are not afraid of your private, hidden leprosy. They will caress you while covering themselves with your infection, and you love them for it. They can stand face-to-face with your ugliness and love it away. They squeeze the hurt out of you by refusing to be offended at your rudeness, selfishness, and hardheartedness. They astound you by being indestructible and unable to be provoked. It is as if they see who you really are and refuse to allow you to convince them otherwise. They remember that love bears all things, believes all things, and endures all things. They know that love never fails. It does not envy, it is not arrogant or rude, it is not irritable, and it does not take into account a wrong suffered. It is not resentful. It hopes all things. It never chooses itself before you. Love will never cease (1 Cor. 13:4-8).

FOR YOUR TRANSFORMATION:

1 Samuel 18:1-3 NLT   Romans 12:10 NASB   Joshua 6:25 NLT

Ruth 1:14-18 NLT   Ruth 4:16 NLT

Proverbs 20:6 TPT   Luke 14:10 NASB

LOVABLE PEOPLE HEAR WHAT YOU CAN'T EXPRESS

Lovable people have divine ears. They hear what you don't say that you need to say. Their beauty is in their ability to perceive the unspoken words of the heart. They probe with compassion. They understand with wisdom, and they know without being told. The remarkable thing about lovable people is that you don't have to explain everything. They have walked in your blood-stained shoes. They have engraved on their souls the scars of being misunderstood, misrepresented, and lied about. They heal with their empathy, understanding, and care. Lovable people hear the hidden pain; they sense the guilt, shame, and hopelessness that you feel. They are your allies without ever knowing you. Sometimes they unravel what you say by defining what you mean. This beauty is the beauty of divine perception. To perceive, you must care. To perceive, you must look. To perceive, you must become a master of the divine senses of the Holy Spirit. Lovable people remember that the Lord hears the desire of the humble (Ps. 10:17), that He hears our supplications and requests (Ps. 6:9). They know that He has given us the open ear of the Holy Spirit (Isa. 50:4). They understand that without hearing, there is no knowing (John 10:3-4). They see the beauty of being heard and understood (Ps. 48:8). They perceive that God loves when we attain to hearing with love and patience (2 Pet. 3:9).

FOR YOUR TRANSFORMATION:

Luke 14:13-14 NASB   Acts 4:18-20 NLT   Romans 12:13 NLT

Romans 12:16 TPT   Romans 13:8 TPT

Romans 14:13 NLT   Romans 15:7 TPT

THE LOVABLE JESUS

"But when he came to himself, he said, 'How many of my father's hired servants have bread enough and to spare, and I perish with hunger! I will arise and go to my father, and will say to him, "Father, I have sinned against heaven and before you, and I am no longer worthy to be called your son. Make me like one of your hired servants." "And he arose and came to his father. But when he was still a great way off, his father saw him and had compassion, and ran and fell on his neck and kissed him. And the son said to him, 'Father, I have sinned against heaven and in your sight, and am no longer worthy to be called your son.' "But the father said to his servants, 'Bring out the best robe and put it on him, and put a ring on his hand and sandals on his feet. And bring the fatted calf here and kill it, and let us eat and be merry; for this my son was dead and is alive again; he was lost and is found.' And they began to be merry.

Luke 15:17-24 NKJV

LOVE CELEBRATES THE RETURN OF THE PRODIGAL, IT REWARDS REPENTANCE, AND IT IS UNREASONABLY GENEROUS AND MERCIFUL—LOVE CANNOT BE JEALOUS OR COMPETITIVE; IT IS AN ENCOUNTER WITH RADICAL COMPASSION, AND IT DRINKS FROM SEEING OTHERS BLESSED!

LOVABLE PEOPLE HUG YOU WITH THEIR PERSONALITY

Your personality is the billboard of your heart. It is the result of the voices you allow to mentor you. Your personality is the movie screen of the things you really believe. The lovable have had their personality cleaned by love's touch. Goodness has stretched its hand and touched their personalities with beauty. The lovable seem to hug the sorrows out of you with their kind eyes and gentle ways. They comfort without having to say anything. Their eyes smile, their face caresses, and their personality celebrates who you are. They never condemn with their eyes. Their gestures are never hateful or mean. There is betterment in their mannerisms. They have had the meanness loved out of them. They are your signposts; they act like your traffic police. They keep you from crashing into the oncoming traffic in others. They are lighthouses of love. They are the personality that everyone knows Jesus loves. You can and will obtain these beauties, for the lovable are all converts just like you. They had to start at the same place, a lump of formless clay in the Master's hand. They remember that the Lord is full of goodness, and they take refuge in Him (Ps. 34:8). They know that their personality comes from their solitary time with God (Mark 1:35). They understand that sweetness comes from the Sweetener (Song 2:3). They see the face of Jesus and are changed by it (2 Cor. 3:18).

FOR YOUR TRANSFORMATION:

Proverbs 12:4 TPT   Mark 10:21   Esther 2:17 NKJV

Genesis 39:4   Psalm 5:12 TPT

2 Kings 4:8-10 AMPC   1 Samuel 18:3-4 NIV

57
LOVABLE PEOPLE POUR OUT THE GIFT OF FAVOR ON YOU

To be favored is to be handed a gift of healing. To be favored is to be vindicated. To be favored is to know you are a credible part of something divine. Favor is God's smile on your obedience. Favor is how God takes revenge on your enemies. Favor retrieves the past and heals it. Favor silences the voice of Satan in your head. And those who give uncommon favor are the lights of Heaven. Lovable people's beauty is in giving to others what they don't deserve but can't live without. The beauty of lovable people is that they have grateful hearts. They know from where all their blessings come. The lovable pour favor on you when you act badly and deserve punishment. They give you gifts and finances when you try to use them or take advantage of them. They come to your aid when you have forsaken them and spoken badly about them. They are God's favor distributors. They remain faithful after you have left them. They hold you with love and kindness in their heart when you have forgotten them. They remember that the blessing of the Lord makes one rich and He adds no sorrow to it (Prov. 10:22). They know that favor is unconditional goodness to a perfectly loved soul (Luke 2:52). They understand that favor is how we silence Satan (Deut. 28:2). They know that without favor, life is a failure (Num. 6:25-26).

FOR YOUR TRANSFORMATION:

Proverbs 11:25 NASB   Proverbs 22:9 NLT   1 Timothy 6:18 NKJV

Genesis 25:6 NLT   Matthew 2:11-12

NASB, Matthew 7:11   Matthew 25:40

LOVABLE PEOPLE LIVE A LIFE OF SELFLESSNESS BEFORE YOU

Paradise is anywhere love is known, and love is defined by divine selflessness. What a beautiful achievement it is for someone to be wrapped in selflessness. And this beauty makes ugliness ashamed. Their selflessness is like being tossed inside of God. Lovable people are beautiful because they can easily say, "yes" to discomfort. Inconvenience and frustrating circumstances do not change their attitude. Genuine selflessness is the sign of a perfectly rich soul. Lovable people have everything, so they covet nothing. They dwell in the arms of perfect love *experienced*. They see a need and run to it—not *away* from it—and we are awed by them. You love them for doing what you should do. Lovable people never choose the best of anything for themselves; they choose it for others. They are calmly detained, derailed, delayed, and distressed without losing their temper, complaining, or showing regret. They are beautiful because they know that God is in charge of their outcomes. They remember to do good, to reward others, to regard the needs of others, and to tirelessly serve others (Luke 6:35). They know that serving is reigning (John 15:12-14). They understand that life is about giving, not receiving (Acts 20:35). They see the heart of Jesus and feast on it (Eph. 5:1-2).

FOR YOUR TRANSFORMATION:

Philippians 2:4   Luke 6:35   Philippians 2:3 NLT

John 15:12-14 NLT   1 Thessalonians 5:15 TPT

Proverbs 19:17 NLT   Galatians 2:20 NASB

59 LOVABLE PEOPLE SPEAK KINDLY AND WITH FORETHOUGHT

The lovable use kind language in the midst of strife. There is no verbal abuse in the presence of love. Love means saying things that heal, not hurt. The beauty of lovable people is that when they can wound, they don't. When they can retaliate, they won't. Kind words define them. You *cannot* provoke them to abuse you during or after a strife-filled situation. They have outlawed verbal abuse, gossip, contention, accusation, sarcasm, and demeaning language. Their words are shocking reminders that true love still exists in people even when they are mistreated, verbally maligned, or have their character assassinated by people who do not know them. Lovable people take joy in repairing the shattered soul. Their words stitch and mend the tears and rips of the soul. They see it, they feel it, and they heal it. They are word doctors—men and women who have perfected the use of miraculous language. They dwell inside of grace, and it reveals itself in the unmerited kindness they show to their abusers. I once asked my mother why she spoke so kindly of people who had stolen from her. She said, "*It does me no good to hate people who don't care what I think.*" Lovable people remember that a word rightly spoken is like medicine (Prov. 25:11). They know that words carry eternity (Prov. 18:21). They understand that gracious speech ushers in the Presence of God (Ps. 100). They see the damage that words can do, and they live to reverse the effects (Prov. 12:18). Their beauty is their healing language.

FOR YOUR TRANSFORMATION:

Psalm 19:14 NASB	Proverbs 18:21 NKJV	Psalm 12:6 TPT
Proverbs 12:14 MSG	Proverbs 15:26 NLT	
Proverbs 1:23	Proverbs 17:27 NKJV	

LOVABLE PEOPLE KNOW HOW TO CHERISH YOUR IDEAS

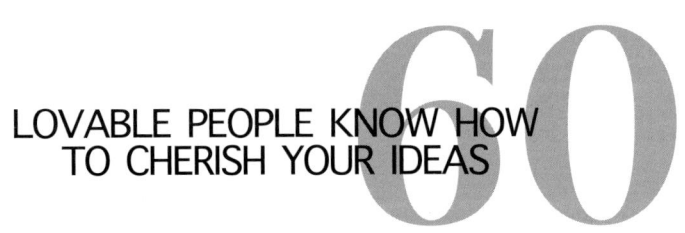

It is a true divinity to love other people's ideas. To make someone feel like their thoughts are special is, in itself, a healing balm. Lovable people make you feel as if you are a genius of thought. They seem to hang on every word you speak as if you are someone special, someone who needs to be heard. They add beauty to you by appreciating the way your mind works. They seem to cherish your thoughts and believe you have something special to contribute to the conversation. They never make you feel like you should be quiet or ashamed of your opinions. They are beautiful because they think your mind is beautiful. Lovable people celebrate your undiscovered creativity. They believe in you in a way that seems divine. They can restore your confidence in your destiny with one word spoken to your insecurity. Their beauty is that their opinion of you is bigger than you are. They see you after grace, love, and Calvary have finished with you. They remember that every God-idea has the power to change the world (Jer. 29:11). They know that hidden within each person is a genius waiting to come out (Phil. 4:13). They understand that life is waiting for each person's destiny to arrive (Isa. 55:8-9). They understand that *there are no normal or average people*. Everyone is priceless and potentially divine (1 Pet. 1:13-16). They see you changing the world with your ideas and long to be a part of it (1 John 4:4).

FOR YOUR TRANSFORMATION:

Matthew 7:12 NLT

1 Peter 2:17 TPT

Titus 2:7 NLT

Leviticus 19:32 NLT

1 Thessalonians 5:12-13

Romans 12:9-11 MSG

Acts 10:34-35 NASB

THE LOVABLE JESUS

And Jesus answering said, A certain man went down from Jerusalem to Jericho, and fell among thieves, which stripped him of his raiment, and wounded him, and departed, leaving him half dead. And by chance there came down a certain priest that way: and when he saw him, he passed by on the other side. And likewise a Levite, when he was at the place, came and looked on him, and passed by on the other side. But a certain Samaritan, as he journeyed, came where he was: and when he saw him, he had compassion on him, And went to him, and bound up his wounds, pouring in oil and wine, and set him on his own beast, and brought him to an inn, and took care of him. And on the morrow when he departed, he took out two pence, and gave them to the host, and said unto him, Take care of him; and whatsoever thou spendest more, when I come again, I will repay thee. Which now of these three, thinkest thou, was neighbour unto him that fell among the thieves? And he said, He that shewed mercy on him. Then said Jesus unto him, Go, and do thou likewise.

Luke 10:30-37 KJV

LOVE SEEKS OUT THE WOUNDS AND BROKENNESS INSIDE OF US, IT REACHES INTO OUR SHAME, AND SCRAPES AWAY THE GUILT AND PAIN OF THE BUTCHERS OF LIFE. LOVE DOES NOT QUIT UNTIL WE ARE PERFECTLY WHOLE!

LOVABLE PEOPLE KNOW WHEN TO SPEAK AND WHEN TO BE SILENT

There is great love in covering people's failures and *not uncovering* them. Lovable people never spread information that damages your reputation—even if it is true. Their beauty is in their sacred silence—a silence that hides you from exposure and keeps you safe while you are changed; it is a silence that gives you time to become *in experience* what you already are *in position*. It is a silence that makes you feel as if you have not made a permanent disaster of your life. This silence refuses to enter into the fleshly actions, attitudes, and behaviors of the old, Adamic man. It says, "I love you. I believe in you. I know you will get better," and, "I love you just the way you are." The lovable are beautiful because they are your caretakers. By their actions, they adopt you into their inner circle. They make you feel like family. They convince you that the best of you is yet to come. Their beauty is in the fact that they are not driven away by the ugly parts of you. Instead they say, "It will pass. This is not who you are." They remember that to cover is to believe in someone's redemptive future (1 Pet. 4:8). They know that whatever you sow, you reap (Gal. 4:6-9). They understand that to be trusted with someone's secrets is a sacred gift (Pr. 11:13). They see the harm in gossip and slander and know its evil source (Matt. 15:19, Rev. 12:10-12). They feel compassion and show it by protecting you (Eph. 4:32).

FOR YOUR TRANSFORMATION:

Psalm 46:10 NKJV   Proverbs 17:28 TPT   Psalm 62:5 NLT

Lamentations 3:26 NKJV   Psalm 141:3 NKJV

Proverbs 29:11 TPT   Proverbs 10:32

62 LOVABLE PEOPLE ARE NOT BIASED OR PARTIAL

Because they have mastered the art of unbiased loving, lovable people are beautiful. All people and creatures are works of art in their eyes. They make you feel as if all the biases of your life were lies. They make you believe that you are truly and beautifully unique. They dig the thorns of bigotry and exclusion out of your soul. They don't know how to prefer one person above another regardless of their past, ethnicity, background, or sins. Their beauty is *healing* beauty. Their open-arms heart transforms, affirms, and restores. Lovable people carry no thorns in their personality or actions. They see you as a perfect beauty, a potentially miraculous person with limitless possibilities. You love them because you trust what they think about you. You open up to them because you are already priceless to them. Lovable people remember that Jesus died for everyone (John 3:16). They know that anyone who does not love does not know God (1 John 4:8). They understand that to embrace is to heal (1 Pet. 4:8). They see that without unbiased love, we are nothing (1 Cor. 13:1-3).

FOR YOUR TRANSFORMATION:

Acts 20:35 TPT	1 Corinthians 16:14	Romans 13:8
Colossians 3:14 TPT	John 15:13 TPT	
Ephesians 4:2-3 MSG	Proverbs 17:17 MSG	

63
LOVABLE PEOPLE REMEMBER WHAT MATTERS TO YOU

Lovable people are beautiful because they have a memory catalogue of what really matters to you. They keep a love journal in their heart. They realize that every person is different and that there are different types of hearts and each one must be loved with wisdom and research. The beauty of lovable people is in their ability to apply importance to *your* pearls, *not theirs*. Their touch is a touch of consideration and forethought. They have loved you in their meditations and their research of your soul. They are not reckless where they walk. They do not break things with their selfishness and presumption. They know that life has created values and priorities and that they should honor what you honor. They should seek out where the pearls are hiding—which thoughts, values, convictions, morals, rituals, and beliefs are pearls to you. The lovable are beautiful because they can enshrine what you enshrine. They can protect, love, and cherish what seems beautiful to you. They remember to look after your interests before their own.

FOR YOUR TRANSFORMATION:

John 6:11 NASB

John 5:30 NLT

John 14:1-2 NASB

2 Kings 4:14-18 MSG

Matthew 10:29-31 TPT

Exodus 2:23-25 AMP

Genesis 16:13 AMP

THE LOVABLE JESUS

"Are you tired? Worn out? Burned out on religion? Come to me. Get away with me and you'll recover your life. I'll show you how to take a real rest. Walk with me and work with me—watch how I do it. Learn the unforced rhythms of grace. I won't lay anything heavy or ill-fitting on you. Keep company with me and you'll learn to live freely and lightly."

Matthew 11:28-3 MSG

LOVE IS GOD IN SYMPHONY WITH OUR HEALING. LOVE IS THE SOUND OF HEALING MUSIC INSIDE THE HEART; LOVE SPEAKS EVERY LANGUAGE AND IRONS OUT THE FINGERPRINTS OF EVIL— IT ERASES THE SOUNDS OF ANXIETY FROM THE MIND!

THE KEYS AND SECRETS TO BECOMING LOVABLE!

Here we have laid out the keys that open the doors of Christlikeness; we go from what to how, we enter the secrets of being lovable. As you read these keys, take time to memorize the solutions, so the fruit will manifest. Fruit is the ultimate judge of who we are, and what defines us, but fruit without process is impossible. We will outline for you, in the simplest terms, what, how, and why we need defining truth. When you learn these keys, you will begin to experience the fruit falling from the trees, you will find a multiplication of spiritual wisdom, shortcuts to relevance, and a map to transformation. For what are we without the clothing of Heaven? What can we offer people if we have no Divinity? What pieces of Heaven can be given away if our tree is bare? Study slowly—chew and digest, until the Bread of Heaven in your mouth becomes the image people see in you!

PART 1

THE TRANSFORMATION LIFE

7 DEFINITIONS OF TRANSFORMATION

Here are the definitions that arise from studying the word *transformation*. From these, we glean needed guidance and direction; these are signposts:

METAMORPHOO

To turn and walk in the opposite direction. Transformation is taking action and believing in the opposite direction, and the result is becoming a totally different person.

METASCHEMATIZO

To expect new encounters. Transformation is the state of expectancy of new encounters with God. The very fact that you're *expecting* a change provokes the Holy Spirit to *create* change.

EPISTROPHE

To see the new you in action. Transformation has the element of seeing. When you're changing, you see the new you in your mind, your heart, your spirit. You can actually see that new person—body, soul, and spirit.

SHUWB

To embrace the pain of change. This is a very powerful definition of transformation because there is pain in changing and you must embrace whatever the pain is for the particular change that God is bringing about in your life. Forsake the you that is only drawn to comfort.

EPISTROPHO

To cease to be the old snake. Since we are changing from one creation to another, sometimes that may be a snake to a dove or a serpent to a lamb. All of these things create a spirit and atmosphere for change.

HAPHAK

To run into the new. The mechanics of transformation are running into the new; as you see something new you run into it. That is transformation: running into the new and despising the old.

STROPHO

To yield to the new momentum. Change has momentum, just as not changing has a momentum. After a time, you will sense the momentum, yield to it, and then it takes you like a mighty, rushing river. Transformation is present when you begin to float on your victories with a momentum that carries you to your desired destination.

THE COCOON

As we explore the Bible, we see pieces of *insight* that lead us to *places of light*. Genesis 35:2 says that we should put away the foreign idols in our hearts that are among us and purify ourselves and change our garments. These are powerful insights: firstly, we must put away the idols of the day—things that slowly creep into the heart. Every generation faces a new set of idols that are designed specifically by Satan to seduce and destroy that generation. These idols of the day are things that replace God by consuming our time. For example, you can see this new young generation is being devoured by technology. Every new video game, hours of social media, and episode after episode of their favorite tv shows steal from their destinies. Ask yourself, *"What could be my idols of today? What eats up my life, my time, my God-given, God-developing, divine-developing time? What devours my attention and steals my destiny from me?"*

All time is a gift for becoming something that contains the divinity of God. God gives us time, and in that time, we're supposed to connect *with* God, live *in* God, serve God, love people *through* God, and therefore be empowered *by* God.

Then we see the word "purify," and its core meaning, this is to remove <u>everything</u> that offends the Holy Spirit. The Holy Spirit is not silent. He makes known to us that which offends Him. However, He entrusts the change to us. So, it says that we are to change our garments, which represents changing our *habits*. When our *habits* change, our *harvest* changes. In the NKJV, 1 Samuel 10:6 says, "Then the Spirit of the Lord will come upon you, and you will prophesy with them and be turned into another man." Here again, the insights are jumping off the page—when God's Spirit comes upon us, we begin to speak the mind of God about ourselves, our circumstances, our families, and most importantly, our present, past, and future. Those words breathed upon by God is called "divine language." They are truths that change us. It is the breath of God and the words of God that become *Rhema* words—present-day, applicable knowledge with present solutions to all of our problems. *The Word of God* spoken over us activates the *transforming powers of the Holy Spirit*. True change happens in our very DNA. Where our DNA is changed, *we* are changed. It is like being born again over and over and over again. With each DNA change, we become new creatures.

For example, in Genesis 32:24-26, we see that Jacob reached the place of self-loathing, which can sometimes be a requirement for change. It became a sacred place where he could no longer tolerate himself. The name Jacob means "deceiver, usurper, supplanter," and we know this to be true by his actions: he stole his brother's birthright. By stealing it, he sealed his reputation and nature in front of the world and "forever" cursed himself with a twisted identity—that is, until the day he decided to wrestle with the *angel of change*. We must do the same thing: we must also wrestle with the angel of change. Jacob said to the One who had the power to change him, "I will not let you loose until you bless me." What is he really saying? He's saying, "*I will not turn you loose until you change me into the man I want to be.*" He refused to settle for a cursed identity, so God changed his name from "wretched deceiver" to "holy Prince with God."

Job declared essentially the same, crying out, "All the days of my struggle, I will wait until my change comes." (Job 14:14, see AMPC) Here again, Job refuses to settle or resign himself to a life he *knows* that God did not create for him to live. He refused to quit at the place of death and ashes; rather, he resigned himself to be the changed man redesigned by the God who promises beauty for ashes (Isa. 61:1-3).

And finally, think about the scripture (Jer. 13:23) that asks if a man can change his spots or a leopard his skin. It promises that we, then, can also do good, who are accustomed to doing evil—through the power of the Holy Spirit.

HOW TO ACHIEVE TRANSFORMATION

Real change is not merely theoretical; there are practical steps to achieve transformation, which must be intentionally chosen for transformation to be worked out and become manifested in our lives.

CRAWL INTO THE COCOON.

How? It's a choice. You must decide that you are going to let God change you. He will, but only if you decide to move out from where you have always lived. Therefore, choose to crawl into that cocoon, and He'll give you the clear instructions, telling you *precisely* what you must do, whatever it may be.

SUBMIT TO THE REQUIREMENTS OF THAT CHANGE.

With every change, God lays out steps and His requirements. Submit to those steps, and you will activate change. Do this anew every day.

DON'T TOLERATE DISOBEDIENCE WITHIN YOURSELF.

When you feel yourself disobeying, rebel against it, defy it, call it out, and reject it audibly with your decided voice: "I will NOT disobey."

SAY YES TO GOD'S PROCESS.

Never forget that you can endure the process if you know the purpose. Say, "Yes," to God's process of change, even if it is sometimes very painful. God is making you beautiful and lovable—a healer. If you keep your heart and mind centered on the purpose behind the process, it's much easier to submit continually to it.

ASK FOR WISDOM IN HEARING GOD.

Pray honestly, "God, I need wisdom to hear you because I'm not sure if you're the one talking to me, or if it's me, or if it's my mother-in-law, or a friend, or someone else. Give me the gift of wisdom so that I can hear you **clearly** and **without discrimination**."

LISTEN EVEN TO DONKEYS.

A wise person makes everyone their teacher. If you only listen to people who you believe are more spiritual than you are, you will not go very far in life. But every person you meet has something to teach you. Consider Balaam, who had to be taught by his own donkey (Num. 22:21-32). Sometimes God hides our answers in our enemies, in donkeys, or people we do not admire.

THANK GOD FOR HIS MIRACLE-WORKING POWER.

Remember to usher in God's miracle-working power, as it is the force that makes all this work. Thank Him, thank Him, then thank Him again, and let the miracle-working power flow.

PART 2
THE BROKEN LIFE

Luke 7:37-50 tells us about the woman with the alabaster box, and here we see the perfect picture of the broken life. This is the place at which we can arrive where all of our self-confidence (in our natural abilities and the flesh) is destroyed by the Holy Spirit or by life and people in life. In this place, we admit our sins wholeheartedly, allowing ourselves to fall at the feet of our Savior. Let's begin with the summary definitions of brokenness. Since brokenness is such a vital part of being lovable, and as we delve into this, we'll be able to open up and peel back the significant meanings like an orange and pull out the sweetness.

7 DEFINITIONS OF BROKENNESS:

As I've examined and studied brokenness, I've found seven definitions that give insight into what a broken life is all about:

BAGA

The undoing of hard-heartedness. This is God removing the hardness of our heart; it literally means that we are to enact Luke 7:37-38. We must accept our past choices, not allowing sin and shame to paralyze us. The beginning of brokenness is to commit to the truth and walk this way, falling to pieces and emptying our hearts at the feet of Jesus, weeping before Him for our sinfulness, breaking before Him—for our disobedience, our self-preservation, self-worship, and *all* of our selfishness. And as we cry out to God for help and deliverance, we genuinely open our hearts and pour them out. This is the undoing. And it's the place of brokenness where hard-heartedness—where the abusers and damages of our lives have made us hard, where the hurt of life has brought us to the place where the only self-defense was not to care and become indifferent—is made tender.

GARAC

The removal of resistance. The broken life is when God removes everything within us that resists something He would ask us to do. This is a beautiful part of brokenness: imagine yourself being in a place where you don't have any resistance against the will of God. Let's say, for example, that you know God wants you to fast for 21 days. Truthfully, in most people, there will be some resistance; but brokenness is when there is *no* resistance, but you have so much confidence in the love of God and what He is asking you to do and in what He's saying that you simply do it.

DAKA

The realization that we need God to live. This is *real* brokenness because there's no confidence anymore that there is any other kind of life or way of life other than His.

DAKAH

Perfect surrender. This is when you get to where you're broken before God and perfectly surrendered to Him, and He is your Lord, your true Master. You look to Him for the cues of life. You pray before you act.

HALAM

The removal of unacceptable vanities. Since we are vain

people—that carry about our pride and ego in our arms like a baby—we need brokenness to purify us. If not, we will activate our vanity and put it in front of others. Through it we will communicate to everyone by seeing, experiencing, and feeling life through the carnality of our flesh. Our vanity may be in our looks, intelligence, or past achievements—or they may have no basis whatsoever, being raw, unfiltered pride with *no* facts behind it. One can have a record of total failure, never having accomplished anything good, live terribly one's whole life, and yet have complete pride and vanity.

HARAC

To know nothing good dwells in the ego. Another part of brokenness is being persuaded that your ego is your enemy, not your friend and that nothing good can come out of egotistical living (Rom. 7:18). You can recognize your ego at work when you get angry, withdraw, reject, monologue speeches in your mind, make vows, or allow aggression to have free reign. These practices may have been your safe place to avoid the hurts of life, but God is a healer. He will teach you to live in Him, and He will be your safety, not your ego's mechanisms.

NACHAH

The removal of self-life. This is <u>very</u> powerful: brokenness can achieve both the death of self and the death of living *for* self in all of its many universes and the awareness of the love which others desperately need. A selfish person plays no part in the healing power of love.

These summary definitions are a diving board to help you into the deep places of a broken life. Let's go deeper still.

> *"And behold, a woman in the city who was a sinner, when she knew that Jesus sat at the table in the Pharisee's house, brought an alabas-*

ter flask of fragrant oil, and stood at His feet behind Him weeping; and she began to wash His feet with her tears, and wiped them with the hair of her head; and she kissed His feet and anointed them with the fragrant oil."
Luke 7:37-38

When we read this story of the woman who was a prostitute, we see that she was literally pouring out her life before Jesus. God can flow through a broken vessel. If we are broken, then the attributes of God can leak out of us. In being broken, the face of God, the love of God, the personality of God, the kindness of God, and all of His attributes that are in the Bible can start outflowing. This is a very important effect; we must not avoid brokenness. Psalm 51:17 (NKJV) says,

*"The sacrifices of God are a broken spirit,
A broken and a contrite heart—
These, O God, You will not despise."*

Therefore, God is attracted to dependence. The broken life is a life of depending on God, relying on Him, leaning on Him. There is a place where our heart is not haughty, not proud, and we depend on God. The *goal of life* is to depend on God, totally rely on Him, and say, "God is my source of *everything*." Psalm 34:18 says that the Lord is close to the broken-hearted and saves those who are crushed in spirit.

Whatever breaks can see God—a broken thing has divine sight. So when God breaks you through loving-kindness, goodness and mercy, you begin to see God in every area and place of your life. You will begin to see and acknowledge His involvement in everything in your life. It is a beautiful part of the broken life. In Isaiah 57:15 (NKJV), God explains it to us this way:

*"[I dwell] With him who has a contrite and humble spirit,
To revive the spirit of the humble,
And to revive the heart of the contrite ones."*

The right self-image ushers in the Presence of God. A true self-image is a beautiful magnet: God is drawn to and dwells with the contrite, lowly spirit. If your self-image is the right one, your life will have the Presence of God ushered in and you will become a conduit of His Presence to other people. You literally will go around walking in life spreading the Presence of God. Isaiah 66:1-2 confirms that the one who God will look to and have favor toward is whoever is humble and broken and trembles at His Word. Therefore, the fear of the Lord comes from brokenness. God is very attracted to those who will fear Him in the purest way and who tremble at His Word. What a beautiful attribute of brokenness—to have so much respect for the Bible, for the Word of God, that you literally tremble at God's Word, hastily conforming to everything it says.

We read in Jeremiah 18:1-6 that He is the Potter, and we are the clay. There is a whole process that goes on when we are on the Potter's wheel. And it is our calling to submit to the spinning of the wheel. When the clay is placed on there, He begins to spin, and then the Potter starts to rip and tear. He begins to apply pressure both within and without. He uses His hands to squeeze the clay and shape it into the kind of vessel He desires to make it. So we, in order to be broken, must stay on the wheel. We must let God squeeze us, pinch us, pull us, tear us, and ultimately, shape us.

Jesus told us that to *the poor in spirit* belongs the Kingdom of Heaven (Matt. 5:3-4). The proper translation of "poor in spirit," is *the absence of confidence of the flesh*. It's simply to say, "I can, of myself, do nothing. I totally depend on God." And to those people, God says, "I will hand you the responsibilities of My Kingdom." How beautiful is that?

And in 2 Corinthians 12:9 NKJV, we read, "My grace is sufficient for you, for My strength is made perfect in [your] weakness." Here again, we have another beautiful insight into God's amazing ability to flow in our weaknesses and make our weaknesses a strength. Most people will hide their weaknesses, but the broken life lifts them up to God. That is the dependence, reliance, and yielding. "Here are my weaknesses, God, and here are my faults, my failures; now take them.

Use them. Do what you want with them."

Jesus told us that whoever falls on the Rock will be saved by their breaking, but on whomever that Rock falls will be destroyed.

HOW TO ACHIEVE BROKENNESS

WORSHIP AT GOD'S FEET WHEN YOU'RE HURT.

It is a fundamental principle that in the midst of pain, you don't want to talk to people; you don't want to have conversations that could dramatically alter your life, but you do want to go and worship God. And in that worshiping comes the cleansing and the healing of the heart. It's only when you are healed that are you safe. Take your pained-filled voice to God, and He will give you a new voice with which you can speak.

FALL ON YOUR FACE WHEN YOU'RE OFFENDED.

When you get offended, fall on your face; don't say anything or talk to people or write things or call people until the offense is gone. Forgive those people. There on your face, talk to God: "Father, I am offended. This is what I find offensive:..." Get *from Him* your plan of action, which could be to do nothing, to admit your faults, to bless your offender, or possibly, He could lead you to distance yourself or even excommunicate yourself from a person. He will always lead you into the freedoms of forgiveness and teach you how to perceive the calling of living like Jesus. Regardless of your way forward, the offense has to be <u>gone</u> because hardness does not achieve the broken life.

WORSHIP GOD WHEN YOU FEEL UNFAIRLY TREATED.

There will be a lot of times in your life when people do treat you unfairly. Maybe someone gets promoted before you, or someone else is given credit for something you did. At that point, to be broken, you lift your hands in worship and say, "God, my future is not in the hands of men. It's in your hands. My destiny is not in the hands of a person, but it's in your hands. I worship you. I trust you, and I believe in you." This is your faith making way for you into the promised lands of a peace that is not stolen by circumstance.

ASK GOD FOR GRACE WHEN YOU CAN'T HANDLE YOUR LIFE.

Many people reach the end of their rope daily. Some people actually live their *life* at the end of their rope. There's no rope—every day, all day, they are at the end of their rope with everybody and everything. This is the time to recharge, refuel, and put gas in your tank. This is when you ask God for grace. 2 Corinthians 9:8 assures us, "And God is able to make all grace abound toward you, that you, always having all sufficiency in all things, may have an abundance for every good work." Ask God for grace, and He'll pour it out over you. Say, "God, pour your grace out over me right now because I cannot handle...(the way my husband is chewing, this smell, the toilet seat being wet, or whatever it may be.)." God is your forever-safe place. This is what Jesus died to give us—intimacy with a God who lifts us out of the miry clays of life.

OBEY GOD WHEN YOU DON'T WANT TO.

This is true worship. Brokenness comes when you don't want to obey God. Brokenness is when you choose His voice over the many running through your head. The highest form of worship is obeying God in what He tells you, *without adding your own spin* to the obedience. Don't add *even a little* bit of your own opinions or ideas to it, and don't dilute it; but simply give it all over to God.

BLESS THOSE THAT ARE TRYING TO HURT YOU.

When someone does try to hurt you, start praying for them and blessing them. It's very difficult to hate a person for whom you pray. This will soften your heart and allow the nature of God to seep once again through the cracks.

GIVE TO THOSE WHO ARE TRYING TO STEAL FROM YOU.

This is the ultimate in Christlikeness: if they take one of your coats, give them the other one. It is a principle of self-release.

TAKE YOUR EMOTIONS 100% OUT OF THE HANDS OF THOSE THAT ARE TRYING TO ABUSE YOU, AND PUT THEM IN THE HANDS OF GOD.

Ask yourself, "To whom do you want your soul to belong?"

PART 3
THE REPENTANCE LIFE

The Repentance Life is a life of illumination and confronting the truths, revelations, and realities of the Kingdom of God. Walking out, living, and trying to create a life requires much help from the Holy Spirit, and that help comes in the form of conviction from Him. When the Holy Spirit convicts you of something, the desired response is called *repentance*. This encounter will happen to you thousands of times during our lives on the earth. To master the repentance life is one of the great gifts you give to yourself, your family, and to God.

Repentance changes your destiny; it changes the fruit you'll bear in your life and the consequences of your life. It changes your relationships, your attitude, your mental disposition, and it changes your direction. See repentance as a rudder on the boat of your life. It allows you to make adjustments in the directions that you are going to reach your desired destination.

Men and women who are blinded by their pride, vanity, and ego cannot repent when the Holy Spirit comes to them. This is seen all over the Bible, such as in Judas Iscariot himself, who betrayed Jesus and was a thief from the very beginning. We read in the Gospels that he would steal money from Jesus' collection. Jesus put Judas in charge of the money so that he could never accuse Him. Jesus trusted Judas in the area where he was the weakest. This was Jesus saying, "Here is your chance to repent from the corruption that is inside you."

All our lives, we will have to repent from the fruit of the Adamic nature, which brings judgment into our lives and into the lives of those we love. Therefore, repentance is a form of salvation. It is a door to salvation, an entryway to all the blessings you and I will ever experience. In becoming lovable, then—as the Holy Spirit reveals to us the ugliness of our attitude, character, mind, thoughts, fantasies, meditations, and actions—rather than caving in and breaking under hopelessness, see repentance as God's mercy. Treat it as a way that God has provided to stop the insanity, the negative momentum, the dangerous consequences, and the diabolical relationships into which Satan wants you to enter.

Repentance, then, becomes one of our salvation blessings. It is what God has given us to be free from the bent, twisted, corrupted DNA we had within our Adamic nature when we were born. Repentance is a place of holiness and a sacred place. It's a place where we can, through our will, save ourselves and our future. So, learning about repentance, how to repent, and what happens when we do, are all *extremely* important.

7 DEFINITIONS OF REPENTANCE:

As we begin looking at these summary definitions from the Greek and Hebrew languages, you will find illumination for your current situations. Your heart will desire the freedom that true repentance brings. Here are seven (7) definitions for repentance:

NA'CHAM

The convicting Presence of Regret. When repenting, there is a regret, but a <u>convicting</u> presence of regret. You literally cannot get it off of you; it is a burden, a rectifying presence creating a desire to change, move forward, and leave the regret that your transgression created behind. This leads to freedom.

SHUWB

To change the mind and point it in the opposite direction. This can be very non-emotional; it can simply be moving to the place where one says, "I don't want those consequences, and I don't want that direction. I'm changing my mind about what I've believed." When you pause and take time to perceive the future that is being created by your allegiance to your Adamic nature, you simply conclude that it is not a future you want.

METAMELLOMAI

Inner loathing for outward actions. As you spend time in the Presence of God and as you spend time with Jesus, the influence and effects of being in God's Presence and in fellowshipping with Him creates an inner loathing for bad outward behavior. Conviction creeps through your inner DNA into the depths of your heart, becoming so strong that you'd loathe remaining the same. You neither want to *be* nor even be *associated with* those actions any longer.

METANOEO

Divine reconstruction of our attitudes. This is a very powerful effect of the Presence, fellowship, and intimate communion with God. Our true attitudes are rebuilt, and they become *the very attitudes of Jesus Himself* concerning the world, worldliness, sin, and sinfulness.

NOCHAM

The re-bending of the will with emotions. In this experience, while repentance is being outworked in us in certain areas, our will is re-bent, reshaped, and redirected. It can be a very emotional experience. We are renouncing the romanticized affiliations that we had, which were tied to the flesh, a part of the very nature of who we became—and so a divorce is taking place. It is a separation from someone who has played a significant role in our lives, someone God has shown us that we cannot trust. We must trust *Him* and crucify our Adamic nature. That becomes very emotional and very personal.

AMETAMELETOS

Transforming light encounters or *meeting and seeing light that transforms us.* To have an encounter with light is a gift to your future. This is the effect of the Spirit of repentance. He shines a transforming light into our lives and we have an encounter that changes us forever: in direction, lifestyle, habits, relationships, attitudes—everything.

METANOIA

To place momentum in reverse. This is what you can call a resurrection of holy desires that immediately causes us to put the brakes on whatever we are doing and put all of our momenta in the reverse in whatever direction we are headed. We stop, repent, and engage our efforts in the reverse direction. This is not passive but an active allegiance to a new direction and future.

Let the significance of these definitions become both potent and transforming as you apply them to your own situations, allowing the Spirit of God to reveal each facet required for your transformation.

Throughout the Bible we are admonished to repent. Many of the scriptures in the Bible talk about repentance and its <u>high</u> importance. The Bible recounts the lives of many men and women who repent, and it completely changes their destinies.

Genesis 42:21 tells us of the moment when Joseph's brothers

repented for their sinful actions against their brother, who had become, by then, the most powerful man alive on earth at that time, after Pharaoh.

In a different time, the time of Moses, the Pharaoh repented, but then *un-repented* because his heart was hardened (Ex. 9:27-35, 12:31-32, 14:5-7). He walked directly into the pain and consequences of unrepentance. We also see repentance in Balaam, who repented for his spiritual blindness (Num. 22:34). The Israelites, who were worshiping a golden calf (Ex. 33:3-6), repented for worshiping false gods and murmuring. In 2 Samuel 12:7-11, the prophet Nathan confronts David in a parable about a man who kills another man's only lamb. Upon David's realization that *he* is the guilty man in the parable (whom he says must be killed), David repents on his face. Hezekiah repents for his pride because of his sickness and was given a reprieve from death for 15 more years (Isa. 38:5). After three days in the belly of a whale, Jonah repents (as I suppose we also would if covered that long in all the digestive juices and stench of a giant fish) (Jonah 2:2-9). And then the Ninevites repent after hearing the message of repentance from Jonah (3:5-9).

Under the preaching of John the Baptist, the Jews began to repent because they felt the truth and the convicting power of the words of John the Baptist (John 3:1-6). This repentance was the gift of God to prepare them for the coming of the King. Their repentance created in them a place to receive Jesus. The woman with the alabaster box didn't say anything; she just approached in the spirit of repentance by crawling to the feet of Jesus, already *knowing* she was a sinner, a prostitute, *knowing* she had thrown away her life. She just comes to Jesus for mercy and gets it—she obtains forgiveness because that's what repentance brings: mercy and forgiveness (Luke 7:36-38). You can never be defeated as long as you're willing to repent.

In the parable of the Prodigal Son, he acts foolish and spends all his inheritance, and ends up eating and sleeping with pigs. The Bible says that when his mind returned to him, his sense returned, and he repented, and returned home. In repentance, he said to himself, *"I'm coming home; I was wrong. That's the wrong life and I don't want to live it. Can I just be one of my father's servants?"* And God, being the way He is, kisses him with affection and love, gives him back the white robe, puts a ring of a covenant on his finger and a staff of authority in his hands, puts the shoes of the Gospel on his feet, kills the fatted calf, and throws a party, declaring to everyone that his lost son is now found (Luke 15:11-41).

Then we have the parable with the Publican and the Pharisee in Luke 18, and the Publican essentially prays, "I am a sinner, God—a **sinner**, sinner, *sinner*; please forgive me." But the Pharisee basically says, "Thank God I'm not like *these people*," and God blesses the one, and rebukes the other. Another great example is Peter when he denies Jesus in Matthew (26:75) and is broken. These are prime, powerful examples of men and women who decide to take God's path to becoming lovable—repentance is the actual secret of becoming lovable; it's the secret of lovability.

Matthew 3:16-19 tells us to bring fruit that lines up with our words. We have all said that we are sorry and did not change in the area for which we said we were sorry. We've all done that. It's part of human nature to seize a truth, agree with it, and not do it. That's because it has not traveled from our mental light to our heart light; it has not become substance within us through meditation and fellowship with God.

Therefore, the repentance life has some *very* powerful truths to consider:

YOUR JOURNEY ENDS WHEN YOU STOP BEING ADJUSTABLE. (PROV. 12:1)

Only a stupid man refuses to be corrected. If he continues in his way, he shall be destroyed. If you stop being adjustable by the Holy Spirit start getting offended at people who correct you or rebuke you or tell you things, your journey is over. You *cannot* become lovable where you are ugly if you refuse to adjust your behavior.

REPENTANCE ACTIVATES NEW BEGINNINGS. (LUKE 15:11-32)

We see this in the story of the Prodigal Son. A new beginning is the fruit of repentance. You can start your life all over again no matter how many mistakes you've made because you're willing to repent.

REPENTANCE SILENCES SATAN (2 COR. 7:10).

When you repent, Satan has nothing left to say. He can only torture you while you're in disobedience; he cannot touch you while you're in obedience. Getting back under the covering of God gives you His authority, the authority of a kingdom that already has the victory, an authority to cast off and refuse every attempt of the devil to torment you more.

REPENTANCE IS THE FRUIT OF GOD, THAT HE CAN RELY ON (ISA. 66:1-2).

God can trust someone who is willing to repent and change. He can *entrust* His wealth to that person.

REPENTANCE EMPOWERS AND ENABLES YOUR DIVINE LIFE (LUKE 3:8).

When you repent, you're empowering and enabling the life that God laid out for you to truly happen. You're not going to have the abundant life Jesus wants for you if you're a stubborn, uncorrectable person.

REPENTANCE IS HOW YOU BREAK THE CURSES OF LIFE. (MARK 5:1-39)

We find this account about a man called, "the demoniac," or what could be called "the ultimately cursed person." 2,000 demons were living in his body—we don't know anyone like this, and we really haven't *heard* of any such person. *This man was a* *mess.* But after Jesus dealt with Him, he fell at Jesus' feet for help, Jesus ordered the demons out, and all 2,000 demons left, and then the Bible says that the man put his clothes back on and was in his right mind. He became a changed person—in full view of everyone.

REPENTANCE PUTS YOU OUTSIDE OF THE REACH OF SATAN (2 COR. 7:9).

Repentance is your safe place. The quicker you repent, the less consequences you will experience.

REPENTANCE ACTIVATES YOUR INHERITANCE (LUKE 15:25).

The Prodigal Son repented and left his transgressions behind. As he walked away from sin, his inheritance ran *to him*. His life was resurrected.

REPENTANCE RELEASES THE PRESENCE OF GOD (LUKE 7:37-38).

The woman with the alabaster box is worshiping Jesus and crying at His feet, and she knows what kind of man He is. She had heard about how He loves lepers, is willing to make contact with them, and cure them. She knew about His delivering Mary Magdalene from demons (it's possible she knew Mary and may have even been her friend.) This woman's repentance released the Presence of God, because as soon as you repent, you're right with God, and His Presence comes back into your life.

YOUR REPENTANCE ENDS YOUR DESTRUCTIVE ALLIANCES (1 COR. 15:33).

When you repent, your direction changes, so your relationships will also change. When destructive relationships exit your life, healing relationships will *enter* your life.

HOW TO ACTIVATE REPENTANCE

The repentance life becomes a place you and I go to find the beautiful pieces of God that we must receive. Repentance heals our personality. It changes our direction, puts us in close proximity to the powers and supernatural Presence of God, changes the fruit we bear, and changes the consequences of our circumstances. It allows us to see the face of and hear the voice of God again and allows us to begin anew in feeling the love of God. So, how can we activate repentance?

DO IT WHETHER YOU FEEL LIKE IT OR NOT.

FIND A NEW HEART FOR REPENTANCE IN PRAYER EVERY MORNING.

DO IT UNTIL YOU SEE THE FRUIT THAT YOU WANT TO SEE.

DON'T LET WHAT OTHER PEOPLE HAVE DONE INFLUENCE WHETHER YOU REPENT OR NOT.

MAKE IT A HABIT TO REPENT AND FOLLOW THROUGH WITH CHANGE.

DON'T FEAR WHAT YOU WILL BECOME IF YOU REPENT FOR WHAT YOU ARE.

REMEMBER THAT REPENTANCE IS THE KEY TO YOUR GOD-FUTURE.

EMBRACE, LOVE, THANK GOD FOR REPENTANCE EVERY DAY.

PART 4
THE VINE LIFE

7 DEFINITIONS OF THE VINE LIFE:

BOW

To enter the unveiling place. As we learn about the Vine life, one of the attributes is *unveiling*. To have this life and get its benefits, we must be transparent, unveiling our inner selves to God. We have to talk to God transparently, telling Him the truth—*exactly* how we feel, asking for solutions and answers, and hearing His voice and knowing Him. It is a completely vulnerable and transparent place, one where there are no secrets.

DABAG

To hold tightly and refuse to let go. The Vine life is a matter of grafting. When God took us and saved us, He grafted us into the Vine. And the Vine is where all of God's wealth is. To embrace the Vine life is to have a close, vital union with God, but for that to happen, and for the changes to come, we must hold tightly to and *refuse* to let go of God <u>no matter</u> what happens in the outside world.

CHUWL

To wait for the transformation. This life is a dwelling-in, an abiding-in, and *awaiting* for transformation; you dwell and stay and wait, which is abiding. It is not a visiting, a touching, or a momentary encounter but a lifelong attitude of waiting for certain transformations to happen. We are constantly connected to the Vine. We experience a faith for the impossible, a constant state of rest in God as we wait for certain transformations in our personal lives, relationships, our families, cities, countries, the world, etc.

CHANA

To dine on the divine. The Vine life is like dining, a true eating of God; imagine sitting at a sizable table with all the foods you like, and God is saying, "Eat all you want, whatever kind of food you desire," but in this case, the meal *is actually God* on whom we are dining. We dine on the personality of Jesus, all of His virtues, the beliefs, truths, convictions, ideologies, conclusions, perceptions, and perspectives of Jesus. Our feast is comprised of His actions, behavior, disposition, and character—all of these are food, fruits on our tables, dishes we delight in, and delicious aspects that make life in God extremely rich. We are to digest the attributes of Jesus that God is serving us so that they become a part of who we are.

YASHAB

To build a permanent dwelling place. Our Vine life affects our natural life. We are constructing a permanent dwelling place for God inside ourselves for God by talking to Him all day, never breaking our conversation with Him—by having a *continuous* conversation with God. And in that unbroken, ongoing, all-day and all-the-time conversing with Him (about absolutely everything, regardless of what the subject is, receiving and hearing from Him), we stay connected to the Divine. This is really *building*. Each time we refocus our hearts and minds on God it is like laying bricks for a house, a storm-withstanding home where we find rest. Picture your intimate and close prayers as finishing the insulation, walls, wood, flooring, electricity, plumbing, etc. This is what it means to build a permanent dwelling place inside the Vine.

KUWL

To cultivate an intimate life. This Vine life's effect is that we are constantly developing all of the factors that build intimacy. For example, these are quality time, exclusivity, cherishing, obedience to God's will, conformity to God's plan, dependence, and creating an addiction to God. It is a deep, emotional, mental, spiritual, volitional, conscious, perceptive life of intimate conversation; and it is a place where everything is personal.

LAVA

To lavish with unhindered communion. This means to truly throw onto someone a communion that is unlimited and uninterrupted. Communion is not always verbal, though it can be, but is the unbroken mental and emotional, *highly* personal fellowship one has with God (without using words). This is the deepest part of Christianity—communion. It's communing with God with your spirit, your conscience, and your intuition. This action of fellowship is laying every area of life at His feet because you belong

THE EFFECTS OF THE TRUE VINE

"I am the true grapevine, and my Father is the gardener. He cuts off every branch of mine that doesn't produce fruit, and he prunes the branches that do bear fruit so they will produce even more. You have already been pruned and purified by the message I have given you. Remain in me, and I will remain in you. For a branch cannot produce fruit if it is severed from the vine, and you cannot be fruitful unless you remain in me.

"Yes, I am the vine; you are the branches. Those who remain in me, and I in them, will produce much fruit. For apart from me you can do nothing. Anyone who does not remain in me is thrown away like a useless branch and withers. Such branches are gathered into a pile to be burned. But if you remain in me and my words remain in you, you may ask for anything you want, and it will be granted! When you produce much fruit, you are my true disciples. This brings great glory to my Father.

"I have loved you even as the Father has loved me. Remain in my love. When you obey my commandments, you remain in my love, just as I obey my Father's commandments and remain in his love."

John 15: 1-10 NLT

As we read through this beautiful verse of scripture, remember that unless we take hold of the Vine life, we're not going to be lovable at all. Nothing about us will be lovable; we cannot forget that *only* the Vine that makes us lovable.

1. THE VINE LIFE UNITES US WITH THE POWERS OF GOD (EPH. 1:17-19)

Being united with His power is what gives us the ability to be lovable regardless of what has been our natural way of behaving.

2. IT IMPARTS THE VIRTUES OF GOD (JOHN 15:1-4).

Thus, the Vine life is one of impartation. Imagine the virtues of Jesus being imparted to you. Abiding is being constantly given a virtue that you did not have.

3. IT HEALS THE INVISIBLE DISEASES OF OUR SOULS (PS. 51, ISA. 53)

Therefore, abiding is also *being healed*—and healed of all the elements in our lives that are diseased, corrupt, damaging, dangerous, disqualifying, dysfunctional, wrecking, bruising, breaking, or destroying. These came through people, words, actions, and circumstances. The Vine Life heals all of them and makes *medicine* for the *disease* so that we become like a medicine to people, a hospital, which is very lovable.

4. THE VINE LIFE CHANGES THE PERSONALITY (GEN. 32:24-26)

Jacob had to live with the consequences of his deceit, being a usurper, feeling the fear of his brother's vengeance. He couldn't stand the life his nature had created, so he demanded a new one. It wasn't *asking and receiving*; it was a *fighting*. He fought through the doubts, the fears, and the inadequacies. He fought against the feelings of exhaustion and the desire to quit. Into the night and the darkness, he fought. It was not until he was changed that he stopped. This kind of fight never leaves you. The victory in a battle like this gives you a different way of walking. He no longer moved through life the same way. He was slower, wiser, and more conscientious. He wasn't a deceiver, selfishly serving his own ends; he was a prince of God, concerned with the matters of His kingdom. This true transformation of personality inspires awe.

5. IT IMPARTS THE DESIRES OF GOD (PS. 37:4)

This verse proves that abiding is a MASSIVELY important part of the Vine life. When you fellowship with God, your desires change. This makes your desires change in fellowship with God. This makes you very attractive in the way Jesus was attractive because you now have the desires of God in your heart, and we follow our desires.

6. IT TRANSFORMS OUR DNA (2 COR. 5:17)

Literally, you become a new person, a new creature. We never need to lose hope; the promise is to be made a new creation. The old falls away, and all is made new. Through God giving you a new DNA transformation, you will truly become a new species of person.

7. IT HEALS OUR DISTRUST (ROM. 4:20-21)

To be lovable, you also have to be innocent and trusting. This comes from abiding in God and His Word. We must experience the faithfulness that God has to His Word. He always fulfills His promises and is always a person of *impeccable* character. When we trust God, we lose the need to defend ourselves, to fight against the opinions of others, and to allow fear to drive us. The peace of understanding enters our hearts and we are free to be lovable.

8. IT HEALS OUR WOUNDED EMOTIONS (JER. 17:7-8)

This is one of the biggest parts of life because we are emotional people—primarily led and driven by emotions. Although it shouldn't be that way, it is for most people. The Vine life takes your roots deeper. The winds and storms of life are not so threatening. You become more lovable when your wounded emotions are healed. When you're wounded, you speak out of pain, and that pain, in turn, hurts people. You say what's unkind and wrong when you're hurting; therefore, to be lovable, you need to go deeper than your present fears and wounds and become emotionally healthy.

9. IT REMOVES THE FEAR OF PEOPLE (PR. 29:25)

How can we be lovable if we're afraid of everybody? <u>We can't</u>. We can't live in the insecure mental dialogue that twists our emotions. Abiding in the Vine is the place of the extraction of fear and the building of faith.

10. IT PLANTS US IN THE GARDEN OF GOD (PS. 92:11-15)

We have the promise that we will flourish as we're planted in the house of God. Being planted means your roots grow. Your roots determine your fruits, but your seed determines your roots. So, the seed you eat creates the roots your drink from, which determines the fruit you *are*. This is a very transformative, potent, and necessary aspect of life.

When we talk about the Vine life, we are speaking of abiding in God, praying and seeking God. Throughout the Bible we see men and women of God who did this. Abraham did. He was abiding when he drew near to God and the angels in Genesis 18:23-32. While in the Presence of God, they discussed the fate of Sodom and Gomorrah. He sought God by constantly praying and asking God, "Wait, what if there are 10? What if there are 5?" He was in this abiding. Throughout the Bible, we are given example after example to daily seek and pray with God.

Psalm 9:10 says, "And those who know your name put their trust in you, for you, O Lord, have not forsaken those who seek you." Psalm 92:2 declares that it is very good for us, "to declare your steadfast love in the *morning,* and your faithfulness by *night*," while Psalm 119:55 charges us to seek God in the night watch. Psalm 88:1 proclaims to call upon God *twice a day*, and Psalm 55:17 ups it to *three* times a day. But David himself said, "*Seven times* a day I praise you," (Ps. 119:164). In Luke 6:12 (*all night*) and 1 Thessalonians 5:17 *(without ceasing)* we are given two examples of the abiding, or how to be the Vine-life kind of people. They are the ones who produce the greatest fruit.

Then we see the manifestations of abiding, such as bowing, kneeling, lifting up our hands, standing, sincere desires and pure motives, hunger and appetite, and desperation for God, His people, and His Presence. Jesus prayed with such fervor that He even sweat great drops of blood (Matt. 26:38-39, Luke 22:24). In 1 Samuel

1:10-20, we watch as Hannah, who couldn't have children, cried out to God and He answered her prayer. David called out to the Lord for deliverance and his cry was heard. Nehemiah prayed and it was granted that he could be the one to rebuild the temple (2:4). Daniel's faith in prayer was heard even from the lions' den (6:21-22, 9:3, Heb. 11:33). Anna was a steadfast woman of abiding and prayer (Luke 2:36-37). And the greatest of all is Jesus, who *constantly* lived this, would go out to solitary places early in the morning, while it was still dark, and pray (Mark 1:35). God directly spoke to Cornelius, the Roman centurion, telling him, "Your prayers and your [generous] gifts to the poor have come up [as a sacrifice] to God *and* have been remembered by him." (Acts 10:4, 30 AMPC).

And throughout the Bible there are other men and women who are constantly abiding in the Vine, consistently dwelling in God—think of Moses, Isaiah, Jeremiah, Judah Eleazar, Solomon, Manasseh; think of all the people constantly seeking God, searching for, running after, pursuing God, needing Him, wanting Him, simply dwelling in and abiding in God. Jesus was constantly doing this day and night, especially for his 40 days and nights in the wilderness (Luke 4:1-13).

Like them, we have ways of seeking God: day after day in a mountain place, a solitary place, in the wilderness, thanking God before eating, in times of distress, or blessing children, for instance. Jesus is the perfect picture; imagine Him calling to God at the grave of Lazarus, consistently crying out to the Lord. These are the secrets, these are the needs, these are the powers, and these are the impartations of the Holy Spirit in abiding in the Vine.

But how can we activate the Vine life?

HOW TO ACTIVATE THE VINE LIFE

WORD ADDICTION

You must get the Word of God in **everything**. You must know it, say it, and have it in your mind. You must get addicted to the lessons, teaching, inspiration, and encouragement of the Word of God. It's *a mirror, rain, seed, snow, water, a sword, fire, a shield, meat, bread, wine, and* **life**. The Word of God is forever settled in Heaven (John 15:7-10). *Live out* Word addiction; get into the Word.

MEDITATING ON THE WORD OF GOD

> *His passion is to remain true to the Word of "I AM,"*
> *meditating day and night on the true revelation of light.*
> *He will be standing firm like a flourishing tree*
> *planted by God's design,*
> *deeply rooted by the brooks of bliss,*
> *bearing fruit in every season of life.*
> *He is never dry, never fainting,*
> *ever blessed, ever prosperous.*
> Psalm 1:2-3 TPT

BEHOLDING THE BEAUTY OF GOD, OR ASKING GOD TO SHOW YOU HIMSELF

> *One thing I ask from the L*ORD*,*
> *this only do I seek:*
> *that I may dwell in the house of the L*ORD
> *all the days of my life,*

to gaze on the beauty of the Lord
and to seek him in his temple.
Psalm 27:4 NIV

COMMUNION LIFE

"And there I will meet with thee, and I will commune with thee from above the mercy seat, from between the two cherubims which are upon the ark of the testimony, of all things which I will give thee in commandment unto the children of Israel."
Exodus 25:22 NKJV

INTIMATE LANGUAGE

All night long on my bed
I looked for the one my heart loves;
I looked for him but did not find him.
I will get up now and go about the city,
through its streets and squares;
I will search for the one my heart loves.
So I looked for him but did not find him.
The watchmen found me
as they made their rounds in the city.
"Have you seen the one my heart loves?"
Scarcely had I passed them
when I found the one my heart loves.
I held him and would not let him go
till I had brought him to my mother's house,
to the room of the one who conceived me.
Song of Songs 3:1-4 NIV

LONGING FOR, LOVING, AND DESIRING GOD

You, God, are my God,
earnestly I seek you;
I thirst for you,
my whole being longs for you,
in a dry and parched land
where there is no water.
I have seen you in the sanctuary

and beheld your power and your glory.
Because your love is better than life,
my lips will glorify you.

Psalm 63:1-3 NIV

CONSISTENCY

"Now in the morning, having risen a long while before daylight, He went out and departed to a solitary place; and there He prayed."

Mark 1:35

PART 5

THE WORD LIFE

Study to shew thyself approved unto God, a workman that needeth not to be ashamed, rightly dividing the word of truth.

2 Timothy 2:15 KJV

The Word Life is *critical* to becoming lovable because it is the power inside the Word of God that <u>creates</u> the nature of God inside of us. This creation occurs by taking the Word of God and eating it, as Jeremiah 15:16 says: "When I discovered your words, I devoured them. They are my joy and my heart's delight. (NLT)" This means we are to chew on it, eat it, digest it, and then let it change our insides, and this is the secret of becoming lovable. All of God lives inside of His Word, so any piece of God you are looking for, any part of God that you want, any personality trait, virtue, wisdom, strength, all kinds of courage, faith, joy, love, or peace that you want in your life will all come from the Word of God. As you (piece by piece and bit by bit) consume, break down, and digest the Word of God, this devouring of the Word of God adds that eternal piece of God to you. And this is how you become Christlike, and (of course) being lovable *is* being Christlike. In this chapter, we are going to look into the secrets of the Word of God, which are the how-to and answers to the *why, what, who,* and *where,* and put ourselves *inside* of the Word of God so we can see those beautiful Jesus traits coming out in our lives.

Firstly, we'll lay out the Word Life's definitions to get the general overview of the life that comes from dwelling in the Word.

7 DEFINITIONS OF THE WORD LIFE:

DUWR

To remain under the instruction of the Word. This dwelling in the Word is to remain under its instruction. Every day of your life, the Word of God has some other life lesson to teach you, and instruction, some piece of light to give you, or a different direction to go.

ZBUWL

To build a dwelling place for the Word's perspective. Dwelling in the Word life to produce a lovable you comes from building—with your daily choices—a dwelling place for the Word's perspective. Let's say that you have your own perspective on a particular subject. Well, you are 1 of 8,000,000,000 people that are *all* individuals and *all* different. Obviously, you are fallible, just as the other 8,000,000,000 people are, but God's Word is **perfect**. It was given by God and breathed on by Him, given to 40 different people who came up with *the same conclusions* over the period of 1,500 years. That by itself is an impossibility in the natural. You must dwell and build a place for God's perspective above your own. You ask God for His perspective on your life in specific areas. You say, "God, what do you think about this?" and *then conform to what He says.*

YTHIB

To sit and be changed. Here is the picture found in Luke 10 of Martha working in the kitchen while Mary was *sitting at the feet of Jesus*, listening to Him teach. This is how you have the Word life, and this is how changes come. They don't come when you're "washing dishes," for instance—caught up in the busyness of life, too anxious to sit at the feet of Jesus. Your heart must make time for Jesus, giving Him room to minister. In reality, because we can worship God in spirit, this can happen while doing the dishes *if* you're communing *in the Spirit*. While washing up dishes you are also in prayer, talking to God, and then changes <u>can</u> happen because you don't have to be *literally* sitting. It means that on the inside, you're sitting and listening to God's Word, waiting for it to change you.

LUWN

To be persuaded without leaving any doubt. It is **powerful** to be literally in the Word life and experience the transformations of being lovable by being persuaded and having *all the doubts* about your life in God, for Him and with Him, *washed away*. And they are washed away by being fully convinced and getting answers from the Word and your own personal, intimate relationship with your Creator. "Who is God?" "Is the Bible for real?" "Is God for real? What about Heaven and Hell?" "Is this my destiny?" "What is my purpose?" "Why was I born?" "Where am I going? And how do I get there?" God will lead you into a doubt-free life filled with answers and purpose. Becoming doubt free is not about receiving all knowledge but rather trusting in the Word and character of God. This removes all the doubts from our lives.

AMAD

To stand inside of—without fear. This is to come to the place in our lives where we have *no* fear. We're standing inside of God's Word. Fear carries a sound to it that reverberates through our lives. His Word, the sound of His voice talking to us about His own Word frees us from fears, bringing us to a new place of peace and love.

ENOIKEO

To be possessed by the wisdom of the light. Think of the potency of that word: *possessed*. To be possessed means *to be taken over by another power*. We want to become "Word-possessed"—to have the Word of God possess and take control of us and make us do what it wants to do. This is a bold, daring, discerning life. To live according to the Word of God in the face of this world's compromise and confusion will make you a lovable person, someone who can shine the wisdom of light so that others may find their own ways out of the darkness. This comes from the revelations of the Word since the Bible is called *light*.

KATOIKEO

To live permanently connected to the mind of God. Here, in this seventh word, we find this beautiful insight: *we can be permanently connected to God's mind.* Imagine your mind being trained to think like God's mind. And what does God say through Isaiah? "'For my thoughts are not your thoughts, neither are your ways my ways,' declares the Lord. 'As the heavens are higher than the earth, so my ways higher than your ways and my thoughts than your thoughts.'" (55:8-9) There is power in putting the Word inside you, meditating on, dwelling on, and living in the Word of God; then, your mind begins to be renewed. Romans 12:1-2 tells us, "Therefore I urge you, brothers and sisters, by the mercies of God, to present your bodies as a living and holy sacrifice, acceptable to God, which is your spiritual service of worship. And do not be conformed to this world, but be transformed by the renewing of your mind. (NASB)"

As we go deeper into the Word life and uncover its many dynamics, such as how to *activate* the Word of God, what it means to be in the Word life, and how that makes you lovable, let's firstly give an overall description of the Word of God:

We know that the Word of God is called a **mirror** (James 1:23), so it reflects who we are *in* God and *outside* of God.

It's also **water** (Eph. 5:26), so we can drink it, and it refreshes and cleanses us.

The Word of God is **seed** (Luke 8:11), so it goes down into us and grows.

It's a **sword** (Eph. 6:17), and it can be a weapon wielded both defensively and offensively.

The Word of God is **rain** (Isa. 55:10-11), watering our thirsty and dry grounds.

It's **fire** (Jer. 23:29), so we know it consumes all the sin and turns that sinful past life and negative nature into ashes.

And we know the Word of God is **powerful, active, quick,** and **sharp** (Heb. 4:12), moving mountains and creating miracles.

The Word is **medicine** (Prov. 4:20-22), healing our body, soul, and our spirit.

It is called **milk** (1 Pet. 2:2); when we are young, we drink it, and it makes us stronger. When we get to the middle stages of life, it is **bread** (Matt. 4:4) to us, and it's **meat** (1 Cor. 3:1-3) when we're fully grown, having become fathers and mothers.

The Word of God is called **truth** (John 17:17)—therefore, God's Word is The Truth, and that truth is what leads us into the light.

It's called a **lamp** (Ps. 119:105) that lights the path and gives the direction we're supposed to go. These are metaphors of the Word of God which teach us how it can work in our lives, inspiring us through our need for light, water, a weapon with which to fight, etc. As we pursue the Word in these ways, we experience its power to transform.

Now we can discuss the different aspects of the Word life and the Word life and how it is so effective in making us lovable. To become like the Word is to become like Jesus, and He is, of course, the most lovable person in all of existence. God hides His Word behind our obedience. So, when we obey, the power of the Word steps forward. God honors His Word in us, so when He looks to answer our prayers, He doesn't look for our opinions. He looks for His Word living inside of us because He knows He can trust His Word and partner with it. When God's Word is dwelling within us, our lives are activated according to the victories and standards of God's kingdom. When we abide in what God has already decreed, He can move in and create change. He pours His power into His own Word, not ours—since, really, the only one God can fully trust is *Himself.*

The Word of God carries the power of God. Therefore, the more we get inside the anointing of the Word of God, the more power we manifest in our lives. It activates the Holy Spirit—when we pray the Word of God, the Holy Spirit is activated and begins to perform signs, wonders, and miracles.

Every Word of God ushers in eternity. Therefore, the Word is the key that unlocks the door between this side and the other side, this earthly side where we live and the Heavenly realm where God lives. This key allows us to travel between the two worlds in the Spirit. The Word of God is the source of all divine wealth, and all the wealth and riches of God are contained inside His Word. So, the more of His Word you have, the more of His riches and wealth you will experience. The Word of God is our armor and our protection. The Devil throws something at us, and we throw the Word at him, and his temptations, seductions, or lies bounce off of that Word and never reach us.

Every thought of God heals something sick inside of us. The Word is the mind and thoughts of God, and when we receive His Word, something sick in our life is cured. Therefore, abiding in the Word of God is the same as abiding in God, which we see in John 15:7-9. God can trust His Word, and when we are full of His Word, He can trust us. Wherever the Word of God reigns, God manifests Himself. Let meditating on this become a powerful and effective part of your life.

Let's examine some of how the Bible speaks about itself and what we are meant to *do* about that:

1. STUDY THE WORD OF GOD

2 Timothy 2:15—we are commanded to the study of the Word to accurately handle it.

2. MEMORIZE IT

Joshua 1:8—Remember that if you memorize the Word, you heal

your mind.

3. MEDITATE ON IT

Psalm 1:2-3—If you meditate on the Word of God, you'll prosper and have great success. When a passage or verse really speaks to you, don't read on; think about it. Pray about it. Picture it. Put yourself into its scenario or promise. Write about it. Spend time with it and develop the revelation into a meal that you can consume. Then praise God anew for it. This is meditating on the Word.

4. PRAY OVER IT

Psalm 119:18—Praying the Word releases great power in your life and will cause you to see what you've never been able to see before.

5. READ IT OUT LOUD

2 Timothy 3:16—There is a tremendous, life-changing effect when you read the Word out loud.

6. LISTEN FOR GOD'S VOICE IN IT

Romans 10:17—Here we're told that faith comes from hearing, and hearing through the Word of Christ.

7. SING IT

Colossians 3:16—Singing the Word activates it like nothing else can; I've never felt anything so beautiful as when I'm singing the Word of God.

8. COMMUNE OVER IT

Exodus 25:22—When you read, you start communing. It starts speaking to you, explaining things, teaching you, and finding solutions—which is *powerful*.

9. JOURNAL IT

Habakkuk 2:1-2—Write down what God tells you because only what you remember has the power to keep changing you.

10. PREACH IT

2 Timothy 4:2—Everyone is called to preach the Word of God to someone at least one-on-one. Whether you're called to do it from a pulpit or not, you are called to preach the Word of God to everyone with whom you speak.

11. DECLARE ITS WONDERS

Psalm 40:5—Start declaring what the Word of God says and your attitudes will change, your fear will leave, your doubt and discouragement will leave, and you will be full of peace.

12. QUOTE IT

Matthew 4:4—This is what Jesus did to the Devil. When the Devil tells you a lie, quote the Bible, and you will destroy that lie.

13. USE IT AS A SWORD

Luke 4:10-14, Heb. 4:12—The Word of God is to be used in your personal battles against the enemy.

14. THANK GOD FOR IT

Ezekiel 3:3—Thank God for His Word and it will cause you to appreciate it more and discover more treasures in it.

15. EXPOUND ON IT

Psalm 119:130—This means to break the Word of God into little pieces and to feed it to people who are younger in the Lord.

16. FELLOWSHIP OVER IT

Jeremiah 15:16—Find your peers, sit down and talk about the Bible to each other, and fellowship over the Word of God together.

17. LOVE IT

Psalm 119:97—Nothing has the power to change us like loving the Word of God. Once we love something, we give it the power to convert us.

18. WORSHIP WITH IT

Ephesians 5:19—Sing the Scriptures and watch the whole atmosphere of your personality and home change.

19. USE IT AS HEALING MEDICINE

Proverbs 4:22—As you apply the Word of God to sick areas of your life, you'll literally watch it become like your life's penicillin.

20. USE THE WORD OF GOD AS A GUIDE FOR YOUR LIFE

Psalm 19:7-14—You'll find the Word of God will always have an answer for your life and a direction you should go.

21. USE IT AS COMFORT

Psalm 119:50—The Word of the Lord is the most comforting force. All my life, in any situation in my life where I've needed comfort, I've quoted the Word of God and found comfort.

22. USE IT AS WISDOM FOR YOUR LIFE

Proverbs 4:7—Follow the leadings and instructions of the Word of God and you will become a very wise and powerful person.

THE 7 WAYS TO ACTIVATE THE WORD OF GOD

1. BELIEVE THE WORD OF GOD—THIS ACTIVATES IT.

2. ACT ON THE WORD OF GOD—THIS ACTIVATES IT.

3. SEARCH THE WORD OF GOD—THIS ACTIVATES IT.

4. RESPECT THE WORD OF GOD—THIS ACTIVATES IT.

5. HONOR THE WORD OF GOD IN FRONT OF OTHERS—THIS ACTIVATES IT.

6. SAY THE WORD OF GOD ALL DAY LONG—THIS ACTIVATES IT.

7. LEARN ITS REVELATIONS AND HIDDEN MYSTERIES—THIS ACTIVATES IT.

When you enact the Word in these ways, it will create the lovable version of you.

PART 6
THE CRUCIFIED LIFE

I have been crucified with Christ and I no longer live, but Christ lives in me. The life I now live in the body, I live by faith in the Son of God, who loved me and gave himself for me.

Galatians 2:20 NIV

This is the perfect description of the Crucified Life. Of the many insights in this verse, the first is that "I have been crucified with Christ." This has *already happened,* so now I need to activate the crucified life into my present, daily living. As you know, you have flesh—an old man, an old nature. You are at war with that old nature day after day. The rebellious you, the discouraged, depressed, proud, vain, unteachable, sneaky, deceitful, lying, lustful, perverted, etc., you no longer have permission to lead. All of these need to be crucified. They can't be suppressed or hidden. We can't hide the behavior even though we are filled with the thoughts. We have to crucify the dangerous and dirty parts of our lives, what's deceitful, compromising, selfish, manipulating, controlling, guilting, seducing, and *many* more parts of our lives.

This principle of the crucifixion of the believer is one of the *most powerful* things we can master. We all have to crucify ourselves daily because we are, at the roots of our Adamic natures, selfish. But our divine natures are selfless. Our divine nature puts others first and looks for their well-being above our own. It is kind, patient, gentle, and gives of itself. This is your destiny. It is the lovable you. Never forget that what you feed grows and what you starve dies. Therefore, we must listen to the call of our divine nature. Then, it is imperative that we feed the divine nature in us. As we put the Word of God in us, we strengthen our divine nature. And as we refuse to listen to the impulses and urges of the flesh, we are starving our flesh to death, and in essence, crucifying it. To become lovable, we must crucify the unlovable parts of us.

As we go into the definitions of the crucified life, these words will give us great insight into how to live out this life.

7 DEFINITIONS OF THE CRUCIFIED LIFE:

PROSPEGNUMI

To fasten our desires and urges to the Cross. This is as direct and quick as it can be. We take our desire that we know is not of God and nail it to the Cross. For instance, let's say you are tempted to eat an entire pie while you are on a fast. You <u>refuse</u> that desire and surrender it to God. Tell Him that the life He has for you is far more desirable than *any* immediate gratification of the flesh. By doing so, you activate faith, nail your carnal man to the Cross, and walk away from that situation stronger.

STAURO

To crucify our selfishness without mercy. When we face our selfishness and our, "I want, I want, I want, me-me-ME," we take charge of that piece of self and crucify it to the Cross. We literally say, "I take this selfishness and I nail it to the Cross without mercy. This is not of God. This is wrong. This is not why I was born again, and I will <u>not</u> serve my selfishness."

SUSTAURO

To see ourselves dead to deadly impulses. This definition is extensive and dynamic because we all have impulses, urges, and instances that arise out of our flesh. Let us say you get offended and have the urge to yell at someone, cuss at them, or become violent—instead, you say, "NO, I will not give in to this urge. I crucify it in the name of Jesus. I do not belong to my feelings. They belong to me, and I belong to Jesus." Every time you do that, you get stronger in the Spirit.

NAASTAUROO

To ignore the voice of selfishness and self-serving. This is another great insight into the crucified life and a solid tool to help us become lovable. Every desire has a voice, and that voice speaks in order to instruct. Selfishness is in our Adamic nature, and that voice tells us to exalt ourselves above all else. As we ignore the voice of behaving, acting, and living selfishly, we learn to become deaf to it. When we identify that voice as the voice of self-serving and selfishness, we come to a deeper knowledge and personal conviction. We don't want to feed the old man and make him stronger than our new man. Therefore, we stop, listen for, and obey the voice of the Holy Spirit. He is always speaking and giving us a way out if only we will quiet ourselves enough to listen.

NEPHESH

To deny ourselves our right to be first. The power of this insight is found in Philippians 2. This is living to prefer others before ourselves, to put others' needs before our own. This *is* denying ourselves. This is carrying our cross and crucifying ourselves. That old Adamic nature will always come on the scene declaring its supremacy and demanding its own rights: "*I have the right to do that,*" "*How dare they treat me like that,*" "*I can do this,*" "*I can live this way if I want,*" and so on. Anger is a sure sign that a monument has been erected in our honor and all must bow down to it. Nebuchadnezzar taught us that. Just pull down the idol of self. Nail that self-absorbed version of you to the cross and let it die.

NEKOO

To subdue our wants and needs in preference to others' wants and needs. Again, this is clearly defined: we deny our wants and needs so others can have theirs met first. Make this a lifestyle commitment, and you will live in abundance. It is the principle of sowing and reaping. You can only harvest from what has been sown.

TELEUTAO

To finish living life as an independent person. To me, this is a beautiful and perfect description of the crucified life. Once we are born again and give our lives to God, it means we give our will to God. Then our independent living, our opinionated life, our, "*I'll-do-what-I-want*" life, and "*I have the right to do my thing,*" life ends. We make it end. Jesus said it best: "*It is finished.*" And that's how we need to look at our independent life (away from God). We are no longer living according to all we learned through life. We lay down our defense mechanisms, rebellion, and striving for comfort. We *don't* get to do our own thing. We don't get to make our own choices. We are no longer disempowered prisoners—we are quite the opposite. We are in love, and that which you love, you will change for and make yourself revolve around it. If we're truly dependent on God and surrendered to Him, and if we're truly going to benefit from the blessings of Calvary, we must yield to the fact that these blessings are activated by our devotion to one another, to Jesus. This selflessness activates God's best blessings, while selfishness resists them.

Therefore, the crucified life is entering into a life of denial while benefiting from the wonders and riches of Heaven. As we look through the Bible, we will begin to delve into the subject of the crucified life and see how it brings change. We will realize that it is *impossible* to become lovable if you are not like a murdering, *daily* assassin of your flesh and fleshly responses.

Now let's examine the 10 effects of a crucified life.

THE 10 EFFECTS OF A CRUCIFIED LIFE

One of the greatest breakthroughs you will ever achieve is perfecting the art of personal crucifixion. To die to self is to live to God. Crucifixion is the power to deny the DNA of the lost man and its attempts to guide your choices and control your future. You will find in these effects revelation containing the basic secrets of dying to self and living for Christ. Yield your whole self to the resurrected life. Drink from the well of the resurrected Christ—become what He is and live as He lives!

1. The dead cannot be seduced (Gal. 6:14). If you're dead, then the Devil cannot seduce you, and this is the power of the crucified life. You're dead to the seduction because seduction requires bait, and bait requires a hunger from those being sought and hunted to eat it. When you're dead to the bait, you're dead to the seduction.

2. The dead have no voice. (Gal. 5:24) A dead thing does not raise its hand and say, "I have something to say about what God is asking me to do." No—we have no voice. We agree with the voice of God, and by our faith in Him, we lay down our own opinions. We don't give our carnal mind, with its carnal reasonings, the right to lead us—or even *speak*. We've chosen Jesus as our Lord and Savior; therefore, we have said that He is both smarter and wiser than we are; He is the Creator of the entire universe. We will not be like fools that believe they can think on God's level and are as smart as He is. We are not of that company—we say what God says and align all that we are to believe and say *the same*.

3. The dead cannot be provoked. (Rom. 7:4-6) If you come across a dead person on the ground and poke that body, prod it, yell at it, or call it names, *it will not respond.* There is no provocation in a dead thing. And the goal of the Holy Spirit is to get us to a place where only the Holy Spirit can provoke us—where we are only provoked by the very things that provoke God. Then all other areas where the Devil wants to provoke us to anger and rage will die. This gives us tremendous power and freedom.

4. The dead cannot be bought. (Gal. 2:20) You cannot bribe or buy a dead person with any kind of alluring power, fame, pleasure, or any other type of influence. You cannot buy them because they are not for sale. If you offer $10 million for them to do something, they have no response—because they're dead.

5. The dead cannot sin. (1 Cor. 2:2) Wherever you are crucified, you are not subject to the temptations and allurements of your flesh. However, if you are alive in areas of your flesh, you *can* be tempted and fall into sin.

6. The dead cannot be depressed. (Rom. 7:4) You can't be depressed since the source of depression, many times, is unfulfilled potential and desires. The dead are unaffected by undesirable circumstances, situations you don't like and can't stand, the hardships of life, financial difficulties, relational difficulties, self-image struggles, and many more sources of depression. So, if you become deeply liberated by the crucified life and thus become dead in your flesh, the variables and anxieties of living in this fallen world cannot provoke you to depression.

7. The dead cannot be led astray. (1 Pet. 2:24-25) No matter what the popular voices of this world declare, regardless of what temptations the Devil puts in front of you when you're *dead*, you're *free* from it all.

8. The dead cannot hate. (Col. 3:3) Hate is something we often feel toward people who hurt us or people we love. Since hate is how we make Satan our pastor, *we do not want to give into hate*—even though we may feel it. We get on our knees and renounce it, asking God to send His love to flow into its place. Once crucified, our deadness prevents us from feeling hatred toward anyone.

9. The dead cannot covet. (Gal. 2:19) Coveting is wanting something someone else has. It is the beginning of thievery. It's wanting, envying, and coveting someone else's wife or husband, life, money, position, career, power, looks, and many other areas others get. Dead things do not covet. A dead person does not want what you have—because they are dead to it.

10. The dead cannot backslide. (1 Cor. 15:31) How can you backslide? Backsliding is going back to the old life: going to bars, drinking, and getting high. It's sleeping around, violence, debauchery, gluttony, rioting, partying, and all of the works of the flesh. You go from the place of *light* and backslide into a place of *darkness.* What is dead cannot backslide. It's dead to the past, to the desire of the flesh, and the visions, dreams, and fantasies of the flesh because it's *crucified.* And this reality is effective as we learn about the crucified life, and it helps us to become lovable.

So how do you crucify yourself?

THE 7 WAYS TO CRUCIFY YOURSELF:

1. Crucifying yourself is an act of your will. (See Deut. 30:6) This means that it is something you have to *choose* to do. You simply say, "I *am going* to crucify myself (in this area)." You see yourself hanging on the cross and dead in that particular desire, and you *don't* allow yourself to come down from it. You will feel the pain of this process and want to get down. Your feelings will demand that you do, but this is where you close your eyes, look into the face of Jesus, and tell Him you trust Him and know He is good.

2. Know that it pleases God when you crucify yourself. In order to crucify yourself and produce a lovable you, there must be a conviction that this crucifying of ourselves pleases God. He is honored every time we exalt Him above ourselves. It is an act of worship. When we draw near to God, He draws near to us. God will meet us in our trial, empower us by His Holy Spirit, and lead us into our victory. It begins with crucifixion.

3. Know that it empowers your inner man and your spirit man. You have to be sure that your spirit man is empowered by the crucifying of yourself. Every time you crucify yourself, you put power in your inner man and make it the dominating power in your life so that you can be Spirit-led, not flesh-led.

4. Know that it is the shortest route to Christlikeness. When you crucify yourself, that's the shortest path to walking in the attributes of Jesus. You may have real issues with a person in your life: they offend you, hurt you, and treat you as if you are trash. You may pray, "Lord, I'm the victim of this person. Everything they say and do bothers me, provokes me and steals my peace and joy. So I'm going to crucify myself. And I'm going to make sure I'm on the path of Christlikeness and remove myself from their reach by crucifying the part of me that is offended at them." This brings you freedom and will take you deeper into the nature of the One Who took the punishment for our sins upon Himself.

5. Know that all powers come from death and then resurrection. When you crucify something, killing it and making sure it dies, there's a resurrection that's <u>going to happen</u> in that area. The old, smoking, drinking, you is crucified to the Cross, and out of that crucifixion comes a resurrection of the *non*-drinking, *non*-smoking, *non*-lusting, *non*-hating you. And you can walk in that for the rest of your life.

6. Know that you are not losing anything of value when you crucify yourself and your flesh. You are serving your best future by removing the compromise or sins of the now. You may wish you could party or have a relationship with someone that is wrong, creating idolatry in your heart, but these are thieves. You must understand this: <u>you won't crucify yourself if you believe you're losing something valuable.</u> You won't go through with the confrontation of it and that's why so many have a difficult time living the crucified life. Therefore, you must *measure the treasure.* Think for a moment on that—if you walk in the flesh, you earn the wages of sin and death, but he that sows to the flesh reaps corruption and death. But he that sows to the Spirit will reap life and blessings (Gal. 6:8). You must be totally convinced and persuaded of this principle to be able to embrace your crucifixion and give up the rewards of the flesh. Remember, pleasure has a reward, but you always pay taxes on the candy you buy from Satan.

7. Remember that God's favor always follows the crucified, not the selfish. If you want the favor of God, it's going to come because you have crucified yourself. The favor of God is reserved for those who humble themselves. This is a great secret and one of the most significant reasons for us to become lovable.

PART 7
THE WORSHIP LIFE

*"You are worthy, our Lord and God,
to receive glory, honor, and power,
for you created all things,
and for your pleasure they were created and exist."*

Revelations 4:11 TPT

The foundation of the worship life and one of the great paths to becoming lovable is this: consistently unfolding yourself and laying your life open before God's eyes. When you dismantle your self-will and lay it at the feet of Jesus, you unlock the secret rooms and chambers of your soul and heart, letting God have access to the most hidden parts of who you are. This is worship—the revealing and unveiling of the self to Almighty God. Here we will learn one of the beautiful sources of being lovable: the more time we spend in the presence of God, the more like God we become. The more time we spend observing God, the more we'll be like Him in our attitudes toward people. The more we gaze upon the face of God, the easier it will be to define Him both to ourselves and others. These are the secrets of worship.

Worship is the releasing of the holy spices of Heaven into our personal lives. There are 12 spices mentioned in the Bible, and each spice carries a different type of healing power. Worship releases these spices into the atmosphere, changes it and creates a duplicate Heaven around us. We simply walk in Heaven, surrounded by It, and by Its glory, power, and beauty as we worship.

To worship totally is to <u>refuse</u> to withhold our choices, our opinions, and will from God. It's to surrender them to God and give Him total control of every aspect of our lives. Worshiping is throwing ourselves at the feet of Jesus, before the throne of God, with adorations and exaltations. It is to magnify God with our whole life: with our choices, words, singing, and love in our hearts. These are the paintings of Heaven, the portraits of worship.

And once we see them, we'll begin to discover all of their beauties.

7 DEFINITIONS OF WORSHIP:

SHACHAH

To allow the heart to kneel. Here is the beginning of worship. Worship is not a moment of singing only but a state of *being*. And that state is to have the heart always kneeling towards God.

EUSEBEO

To obey when you don't want to. Obedience, when your will is not in line with obeying, becomes a manifestation of worship.

SEBOMAI

The unity of the cells in worship. There comes the point in a man or woman's life when they have entered a lifestyle of worship, where their DNA joins in the singing and worship. It is literally a place of Divine exchange where our very cells are singing. Each cell sings a separate worship song, making a symphony of our life before God.

THERAPEUO

To cherish with worship and to surrender the self in adoration. Here, again, worship means to treasure God by surrendering ourselves, and becoming besotted by who God is and what He has done. May we always magnify Jesus for all He went through for us.

DOXA

To dive into adorations. This is where our being, our body, soul, and spirit engage worshiping in their different ways. The **body** worships God by becoming a temple, which means what we *do* with our body honors God—what we do with our eyes, ears, hands, and feet, becomes an act of worship. The **soul** worships by what we choose with the will, what our mind thinks and meditates upon, and what our emotions surrender to; these are acts of worship. The **spirit** is the state of our *conscience*, which is hopefully clear and clean, and holy. Our *intuition* is how we perceive God (our perspective and perception of God)—these should be worship. And *communion* is how we fellowship with God in words that cannot be uttered, only known, experienced, felt, tasted, and drunk.

SEBAZOMAI

To love beyond the limits of the mind. Therefore, worship is bigger than thinking; when entered into, worship is a state of existence where we have a reality in which worship is loving God beyond the limits of our minds. In this place, the limitations of our humanity no longer count. We go beyond the limitations of our minds, and we enter the Holy of Holies, the sacred places of God.

LATREUO

To minister to God with obedience and surrender. At the end of the day, our lives are a constant ministry to God. This is shown by how we live them and conform them to the will of God.

We must enter into knowing the worship life <u>through Scripture and revelation.</u>

1. Revelations 4:11 KJV

"Thou art worthy, O Lord, to receive glory and honour and power: for thou hast created all things, and for thy pleasure they are and were created."

First of all, for worship to make us lovable, worship must be a *lifestyle*, not a weekly choice. It must be a *daily existence*. We were created for the pleasure of God, or, we may *bring* pleasure to God by living a worship life. Everything about what we say, do, our habits, and how we treat others and ourselves is either an act of worship or disobedience. Then, as we fulfill this Scripture, we are truly *created* to bring pleasure to God through worship.

2. John 4:24 NKJV

"God is Spirit, and those who worship Him must worship in spirit and truth."

Salvation comes to our spirit. Jesus resurrected that which was dead and under sin so that we can access God at all times. His abiding Presence is always within reach. This is a beautiful revelation and insight into the worship life: it's not just singing, but being *connected*. Two people could be singing in the church: one with their mind, and the other in spirit—having an attitude of loving and adoring God while they sing. The blood of Jesus is never more precious than when we get to enter into the Holy and Sacred Presence of God.

3. Psalm 29:2

"Give unto the Lord the glory due to His name;
Worship the Lord in the beauty of holiness."

Worship must be combined with holiness. Worship with immorality is not worship; it's an abomination. Worship with disobedience is not worship; it's an abomination. But worship in the beauty of holiness becomes *true* holiness. Therefore, worship <u>cannot be disconnected from holiness</u>. Holiness with worship is **true** worship.

4. Psalm 81:10

"I am the Lord your God, who brought you up out of the land of Egypt. Open your mouth wide, and I will fill it."

In this passage, God tells us to open our mouths wide, and He will put divinities inside of our mouths that will sound like the most beautiful music in the ears of Heaven.

5. Psalm 86:9 NASB

"All nations whom You have made will come and worship before You, Lord, and they will glorify Your name."

We must understand this about worship: every nation created, at one time, will bow their knees to God and worship Him. As it says about the name of Jesus, "that at the name of Jesus every knee will bow, of those who are in heaven and on earth and under the earth, and that every tongue will confess that Jesus Christ is Lord, to the glory of God the Father," (Phil. 2:10-11).

6. Psalm 99:5

"Exalt the Lord our God; worship at his footstool! Holy is he!"

Here again, we see that God's very name *is* Holy. He is a God of love, He is truth, and He is holy. If we are to be holy, we must be in His Presence. Consider again: "*Exalt God; worship at His footstool. Holy is He!*" Hence, there is a position of worship. That position is *at the feet of Jesus*. We see this in the story of the woman with the alabaster box in Luke 7:37-38. As she threw herself at the feet of Jesus, she was not rejected or cast out, though she was a prostitute and unclean. *Her worship cleaned her.* Her worship and adoration of God in sincere surrender to Him cleaned her of her impurities. "*Holy is He.*" Getting close to God and His feet cleanses us and makes us holy.

7. Psalm 138:2 NKJV

"I will worship toward Your holy temple, and praise Your name for Your lovingkindness and Your truth."

The focus that we give in a worship life is to constantly thank God for His love, kindness, and truth towards us. If you ever want to rise above the discouragements of life, enter into the Presence of the God of truth. He sees beyond our limitations, flaws, mistakes, doubts, and sin. He looks into His divine purpose in making us who we are and speaks to that place in us. Worship, worship, worship, for as we do, He unlocks His kindness, mercy, and the truth by the Holy Spirit.

8. Psalm 100:2 and 4

"Come into his presence with singing! Enter his gates with thanksgiving, and his courts with praise!"

Here are the three levels: *thanksgiving, praise, and singing*—think of these as the Tabernacle's three locations: the *Outer Court, the Inner Court, and the Holy of Holies*. We offer **thanksgiving** for all that Jesus sacrificed on our behalf, and then we go through that sacrifice into the Inner Court, which is **praise**. We praise Him for the specific things He has done. We recall His blessings and personally praise Him for them. And then we enter His **Presence** and begin to **sing** of all His glories—the glories of *who God is*. These we sing about and *will* sing for all of eternity, as even **all of eternity cannot exhaust the holy glories of God**.

9. 2 Chronicles 5:9-14

As you read this passage, notice how the 120 worshipers got together to blow trumpets and sing in worship, and the Bible says it became like one voice, one sound. And at that point, when all are united, making one voice and sound, this unity opens Heaven, and the clouds of glory descend upon us, and we are literally covered in the glory of God. We cannot even stand up then. Everything created *must* fall on its face and give glory to God.

10. Exodus 15:21

"Sing to the Lord, for he has triumphed gloriously; the horse and his rider he has thrown into the sea."

Over and over we sing unto the Lord because He has defeated Satan on *every* level, in *every* area, in **everything**.

11. Zechariah 2:10 NKJV

"'Sing and rejoice, O daughter of Zion! For behold, I am coming and I will dwell in your midst,' says the Lord."

Here is the purpose of God, His heart, and His motive: He wants us to worship Him so He can dwell in our midst. We worship God for who He is and what He has done, and He comes and builds a tabernacle around our life. Then He sits upon the throne of and over our lives, and we can spend the rest of our lives adoring God and the beauties of God, and all He has done.

With each veil that we remove in this chapter of worship, with each revelation, we see the effects of worship upon us. These effects make us lovable.

THE EFFECTS OF WORSHIP:

1. WORSHIP UNTIES THE SOUL.

When you begin to worship, the knots, pressure, and stresses of your soul *leave*.

2. WORSHIP UNVEILS THE BEAUTY OF GOD.

As we worship, we begin to see the beauties of God that cannot be expressed with words or written with language.

3. WORSHIP PAINTS THE FACE OF GOD.

There is nothing so beautiful in all of creation as the face of God. 2 Corinthians 3:18 explains, "And we all, who with unveiled faces contemplate the Lord's glory, are being transformed into his image with ever-increasing glory, which comes from the Lord, who is the Spirit." (NIV)

4. WORSHIP HUMBLES THE SOUL BY ENLARGING GOD.

When we worship God in the ways we have described and humble ourselves before God, He becomes bigger and bigger.

5. WORSHIP SEES THE GLORY OF GOD.

There is a place where we begin to see the glories of God and we are undone.

6. WORSHIP REDEFINES THE INNER MAN.

While worshiping God, our insides are rewritten, redesigned, and recreated. Think of God as the Architect and He designs us like a building. Remember, this isn't just about singing. You are entering worship when you humble yourself before God, seeking to please and honor Him. This can happen during your everyday life—amid struggles, when overcoming, when exercising. Practice the life of always inviting God into your situation, and you will become your best self.

7. WORSHIP UNLOADS THE SOUL FROM CARE.

Worship is the place of unloading, so as you worship, the cares of your life shrink to the true size that they are before God—weightless. The Presence of God always holds an invitation to cast your cares upon Him.

8. WORSHIP FILLS YOUR HEART WITH GLORY.

In worshiping the Lord, He takes His glory and pours it into our being and we become a tabernacle for the praise and glory of Heaven. And at that point, we are lifted into the Heavenly realms.

9. WORSHIP ALIGNS THE HEART.

While we worship, our heart becomes aligned. Life presents many paths. Every day is filled with directions. We need worship if we are to remain in line with God. To live with an aligned heart is to become very lovable.

10. WORSHIP PLACES US IN THE CENTER OF HEAVEN.

This world comes with stress, fear, pain, sorrow, grief, torture, intimidation, torment, bondage, and hell. Worship removes us from the center of the earth and the world and places us in the center of Heaven, where all is lit by the face of—and the glory on the face of—Jesus. He is the light that fills Heaven. Worship causes excellent beauty and great glory to come into our lives and the wonders and beauties of Heaven are revealed.

We will end with how to activate worship so that we can become more lovable.

ACTIVATING BEING LOVABLE THROUGH WORSHIP

1. *Open your mouth and begin to praise*—and it is as simple as that.

2. *Surrender your will to obedience.* Every time you're faced with a disobedience, answer it with an obedience.

3. *Fall on your face and surrender.* Make this a habit on a daily basis. When your will crosses God's will, fall on your face and surrender.

4. *Honor God's will above your own.* Teach yourself how to honor God's will and put His will first. Learn what His will is in every area of your life and exalt it.

5. *Sing until you feel yourself disappear.* Refuse to stay bound to anxiety and stress. Focus on Jesus; He must increase and we must decrease.

6. *Sing in total trust and faith in God's sovereignty over your life.* When you walk in this faith, your heart actually wants to express itself with singing and gratitude.

7. Lift your hands and you will lift your heart. Do this as you adore all of the beauties that make and define God.

PART 8
THE DECISION LIFE

> *""Now therefore fear the Lord and serve him in sincerity and in faithfulness. Put away the gods that your fathers served beyond the River and in Egypt, and serve the Lord. And if it is evil in your eyes to serve the Lord, choose this day whom you will serve, whether the gods your fathers served in the region beyond the River, or the gods of the Amorites in whose land you dwell. But as for me and my house, we will serve the Lord.""*
>
> Joshua 24:14-15

We begin with this scripture because it's the perfect verse for explaining the Decision Life. Here Joshua is faced with a mixed multitude of people, among which are some who want to go into the Promised Land, and some who want to go back to Egypt. Some want to serve God and some do not want to serve Him. Some love Him and others hate Him; some believe in Him and some doubt Him. This brings Joshua to say to them, in essence, "This is *my decision*: as for me and my house, we will serve the Lord." Therefore, the **decision life** becomes the **apex**, the center of *all Christianity*. Nothing can happen *without a choice*, and as human beings, it is said that we make an average of 30,000-35,000 per day.

Every choice you make, conscious and unconscious, leads to some sort of consequence. Decisions are extraordinarily powerful, and in order for us to become lovable, we will have to, many times, choose to *be* lovable when we don't *feel* lovable. We will have to choose to love when we feel like giving pain to someone. We'll have to choose to be kind when we want to be mean. We'll have to choose to speak kindly when we want to speak ugly and damaging words.

Decisions, therefore, become the essence of all of the places of holiness that we'll ever occupy. Decisions are at the center of who we are and what we will be. There is no escaping the reality that all of life is a *choice*. And God has given us the most sacred responsibility of all, which is free will. Free will, then, is the best and the worst of everything. Free will is a blessing if we give it back to God. But free will used to serve the flesh—the ego, pride, vanity, lusts, disobediences, rebellion, debauchery, worldliness, and demonic life—that becomes the place of destruction.

Let's begin with these definitions to know what God means when He tells us in Deuteronomy 30:19, "I call heaven and earth to witness against you today, that I have set before you life and death, blessing and curse. Therefore choose life, that you and your offspring may live," (forever with God).

7 DEFINITIONS OF THE DECISION LIFE:

CHARATS

To select the divine. The decision life, which is the divine decision life, is the perfecting of making divine choices. God teaches us to perfect our selections. He teaches us how to look beyond the natural and select His higher way. There is always a choice either for the divine or the disastrous, and we are trained by the Holy Spirit to choose the divine.

CHARUNTS

To diligently choose the sacred. Diligence, then, becomes an active ingredient of the divine will. Diligence means the *continual and consistent habit* of obeying and choosing the sacred above the profane and the corrupt. It is deeper than motivation or feelings. Diligence comes from a conviction.

EKLEGOMAI

To examine with divine eyes. Choices, for a believer, become an examination before a decision. We learn to examine everything before we act. And we use divine eyes. What does this mean? We do not examine with *our* intelligence, opinion, bias, or prejudice. We only examine with divine eyes: "What would God *do, think, or say* in this situation?"

BACHAR

To train the will to prefer divinity. This is a training, a discipling, and an apprenticeship of preference. It is to constantly choose to create a routine where what is divine is your preference. Divinity, which is *an attribute or virtue that comes out of the nature and personality of God,* becomes the focus of that for which you are looking.

BARAR

To examine the outcome. It is powerful to value your life so much that you take the time to consider the outcome before you make the decision. We are always teaching ourselves how to think with God's mind <u>before</u> we make a decision because every choice will yield either a *blessing* or a *curse* outcome.

BAR

To empty the heart of selfish choosing. This is one great aspect of divine-decision living: to acknowledge that our heart is full, it has drawn conclusions, developed behavioral mannerisms, and has concerns, fears, and carnal desires. When we learn how to empty our hearts of selfishly choosing, we enter into the realm of being lovable.

MIBCHAR

To delight in agreeing with God. The ultimate fruit of a trained, sanctified, purified will is *enjoying* and *agreeing with* God. You will find living this out will become extremely powerful.

As we go now into the meat of our decisions and choices, we begin with this reality that is found in Deuteronomy 30:19, that God has set before us life and death, blessing and curses. **Every choice yields a harvest** (Gal. 6:7-9). Every decision is a *sowing* and there will be a similar kind of *reaping.* For example, when we choose to overeat for years and years, our harvest is being overweight, possibly experiencing problems with diabetes, heart, arterial issues, blood pressure, problems in our veins, thyroid, kidneys, and liver—and this is all because of the *choices* we make to put pesticides, chemicals, metals, and poisonous substances into our bodies. We must learn that *every choice leads to a harvest.* Every choice leads to a destination. We are headed to destinations because of *our will* and *choosing.* We can see this in the lives of Adam and Eve in Genesis 3:1-4.

Adam and Eve had the tree of the knowledge of good and evil in their garden, and God essentially said, "Do not eat it, or you will die," (2:16). The serpent deceived Eve, but Adam disobeyed what he already *knew* to be true, and this is what happens in our lives. When we compromise, we end up in places we didn't realize we would. This is the danger of making decisions without knowing the destination of that decision. We see that choices define our destinies. Joseph shows us this. (Gen. 31:12-13).

Joseph was pursued by the wife of Potiphar, his boss—his wife lusted after Joseph and tried to seduce him over many days, but his response was always, "No, no, NO." She finally attacked Joseph and as he fled away, she ripped his cloak off of him (he ran away naked.) She kept his cloak and created a story of deceit and entrapment. As a result, Joseph ended up in prison, but God promoted him because he made the right choice even from prison. And He can do the same with you: even from a jail that's the outcome of a godly choice, or a restriction arising from a godly decision made, God can promote and bless you. But bad choices end Godly deliverance. Every desire breeds a hunger.

In Mark 5:1-7, we read of a man who made so many bad choices in his life that he is called "The Demoniac." He opened himself up to *over 2,000* demon spirits, making so many poor choices in his life that demons entered. Our choices open us up either to the demonic or to the holy. This man had 2,000 demon spirits living in his body; every choice he made created and enlarged his desires and hunger for evil, for darkness. So every choice, every decision opens doors and closes doors. Genesis 39:1-6 proves this: as Joseph was continually making the right decision—while under betrayal, rejection, abandonment, hurt, and pain, and when he was wounded, hated, unwanted, cast aside, and sold as a slave by *his own brothers*—he closed doors to bitterness. Decisions open doors. Joseph chose to make the best out of every decision and every circumstance. *He chose* to be a man of God. His circumstances certainly didn't dictate this decision; he chose *despite* the pain, rejection, and betrayal he felt. As we *choose* to be men and women of God in horrible situations, God finds a way to give us favor and open godly doors.

Therefore, we see that **decisions activate Heaven or Hell.** In Exodus 32:1-5, we observe the account of the Israelites building a golden calf (worshiping an idol) when God came down, opened the ground, and swallowed the Israelites up into Hell because they decided to activate Hell. We also see many in the Bible activate Heaven—Jesus activated Heaven every day. Many of the disciples activated Heaven by their choices. They chose to disobey their flesh, their selfishness, and demons and chose to listen to the Holy Spirit, doing all He said.

Decisions are the key to our inheritance. Ruth teaches us this principle because she was pagan; yes, she was married to one of Naomi's sons, but she was still from a wicked country and tribe. She was a Moabitess, and they were descendants of Ham. Remember, decisions are like a key that unlocks our inheritance, whether for good or evil. Ruth basically said to Naomi, "Do not depart from me. I want to follow you. Where you go, I will go. Your God will be my God. Your house will be my house." She *decided* not to go back to the heathen tribe she was from, with all of its curses, but instead to go with

Naomi, an Israelite. She chose the path of God and will be forever remembered for it.

A choice is the ultimate freedom. God gave us the right to choose, and it is the ultimate freedom. But if we do not manage our choices with Godly wisdom, we end up suffering—sometimes for the rest of our lives. Think about how many parts of your life are the fruit of a bad choice. And if you could go back and re-decide and re-choose, how much in your life would you change?

Esther faced this reality when she had a choice to make, and it meant life or death, but to save her people, she had to take on that risk (Est. 4:16). This makes her words some of the most beautiful in the Bible: "If I perish, I perish." This commitment to a godly choice delivered her people. She gave them hope and changed the course of history. Esther went in to see the king—when going without being summoned by the king could cost you your life. He had to extend the scepter of favor, which he did. That choice she made saved her nation and her people and saved all of us as well.

Life is an addiction to choices. Again, the Demoniac in Mark 5 shows us that he continued for years and years in a state of addiction to bad choices. He found himself in a graveyard, chained up, and so deeply troubled that the Bible says he ran around naked in that graveyard day and night, screaming, tortured, yelling in torment, and cutting himself. When people tried to restrain him with chains, he burst the chains like they were strings. The demons gave him supernatural strength, and every demon leads to some form of insanity.

We become what we choose. The woman with the alabaster box in Luke 7:37-42 demonstrated this because she became something other than what she was. By reputation, we know that she was a prostitute. We also know she brought an alabaster box that was worth one year's salary, which in her case was from her occupation of prostitution, the money she made selling herself. She brought all she had, which was ashes, but she still brought everything to God, laying it at Jesus' feet. By this she said, "This is all I have, and this I give to you." This decision changed *who she was. Jesus* spoke about her that as long as there is time, her sacrifice for Him would be preached, proclaimed, and declared throughout the whole world. Imagine that: the one choice she made to see Jesus that day made her eternally famous. We are famous for the choices we make. Whether our reputation is with family and friends or goes into spheres of influence, our choices teach people who we are.

Divine choices align us with our blessing and fleshly choices align us with a curse. After all, observe Caleb as we read about him in Joshua 14:12-15, where Caleb asks Joshua (by actually saying), "***Give me***" the mountain Hebron—meaning "the place of intimate fellowship with God"—for which he'd been waiting 40 years, and which was promised to him as his possession. And Joshua replies that Caleb has earned it, and charges him to go get his mountain. So, he went to the mountain of Hebron, which giants possessed, and Caleb killed them, took possession of it, and gave that inheritance to his children. Divine choices align us with a blessing or with a curse.

Achin, when they went into the Promised Land, stole some of the garments items taken when they conquered places, which was not allowed. Because of his decision, he and his family were killed and thrown into a pit.

All greatness is a continual choice. If you want to be great in the eyes of God, the Bible says, "The greatest in the Kingdom is the servant of all," (Matt. 10:26-28). Jesus taught us that to be great, we must serve people. We must choose to treat people as if they are more important than we are. We must choose to honor others above ourselves. We must choose to prefer people before we prefer ourselves, which we are commanded and encouraged to do in Philippians 2:3-4 and Acts 10:38.

These all reveal to us the power of the decision life. To be lovable, we must master choices. We must master decision-making, the art of divine choosing. This enables us to cast out of our lives every area that is not Christlike. All ugly behaviors, available to Satan's manipulation, the fruit of all demonic choices, and the driving pain of rejection will no longer rule us. We become lovable because we decide to become lovable. This is a wise decision that counts the cost of transforming our will.

HOW TO ACTIVATE THE WILL TO BECOME LOVABLE:

1. Decide without doubting your choice—Jesus did this (read Hebrews 12:1-2.) It says that He chose the agonies and pains of the Cross for the joy that was set before Him. He did not doubt His choice.

2. Choose the will of God—We see Jesus enacting this in Luke 22:42 when He says, "Not my will, but yours be done."

3. Purify your motives—Philippians 2:3 commands us to do <u>nothing</u> out of impure motives but with a sincere and authentic heart. Purifying your motives is the essence of choosing Godly things. To be lovable, let's take a deeper look into ourselves. What is driving us? We must purify our motives, aligning our hearts with God's, before making our choices.

4. Ask for wisdom when choosing—James 1:5 NIV says, "If any of you lacks wisdom, you should ask God, who gives generously to all without finding fault, and it will be given to you." So, ask God for wisdom; pray, "Give me wisdom, God. Show me the steps of wisdom, and how to choose the lovable behavior above the miserable behavior."

5. Pray for insight—Just like Hezekiah prayed to God: "Help me, teach me, show me what I should do, and open my eyes. Open my heart; let me see what you want me to do" (1Kings 3:10). Pray for insight; ask God for the Spirit of revelation and wisdom, as found in Ephesians 1:17-19. Remember, you do not want to be someone who pushes people away. This is how we are naturally. Therefore, pause and pray. We need to see with the eyes of our Father.

6. Once you know what is right, do not hesitate to do it—Jesus said in Mark 11:23 (KJV), "For verily I say unto you, That whosoever shall say unto this mountain, Be thou removed, and be thou cast into the sea; and shall not doubt in his heart, but shall believe that those things which he saith shall come to pass; he shall have whatsoever he saith." We must be very careful not to doubt, not to hesitate in doing what God has revealed that we should do. Don't reason with your sentiments—just follow God's leading if you want God's outcome.

7. Trust God with your whole heart—Psalm 125:1-2 promises, "They that trust in the Lord shall be as mount Zion, which cannot be removed, but abideth for ever. As the mountains are round about Jerusalem, so the Lord is round about his people from henceforth even for ever," (KJV). The final act at the end of the day is to trust God. Every time you choose, trust God. With every decision, trust God. Every time you do what God wants you to do (even when you don't want to), trust God—for the essence of a lovable life is to trust God.

MORE FROM IVAN

IVAN'S STORE

Find more of Ivan's great resources from his best selling books to messages and workbooks.

IVAN'S APP

Stay connectd with free messages and insights into Ivan's ministry.

IVAN'S ORPHAN MINISTRY

BECOME A PARTNER

James 1:27 calls us all to represent God's love and blessings to orphans and widows. This is the path of purity and blessings. Become a Monthly Partner!

MEET OUR ORPHANS

Ivan founded a higher education orphan community in Guatemala. Meet the children who have been rescued and read their incredible stories.

 WHAT MATTERS
ministries and missions

Help
RESCUE GOD'S
Children

According to Psalm 68:5, God is the Father of all orphans. As He guides and guards your family, join us in rescuing His children: the orphan and widow!

WHATMATTERSMM.ORG
MAKE A DONATION OR BECOME A MONTHLY PARTNER TODAY!

James 1:27
"Pure and genuine religion in the sight of God the Father means caring for orphans and widows in their distress and refusing to let the world corrupt you."
NLT

Thank you!